Poems for the Great Days

POEMS *for the*

GREAT DAYS

Compiled by

THOMAS CURTIS CLARK *and*
ROBERT EARLE CLARK

Granger Index Reprint Series

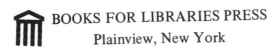 BOOKS FOR LIBRARIES PRESS
Plainview, New York

Copyright 1948 by Stone & Pierce
Reprinted 1973 by Arrangement with
Abingdon Press

Library of Congress Cataloging in Publication Data

Clark, Thomas Curtis, 1877-1953, comp.
  Poems for the great days. comp. by Thomas Curtis Clark
and Robert Earle Clark. Plainview, N.Y., Books for Librarie
Press [1973, c1948] 245 p. 23 cm.
(Granger index reprint series)
Reprint of the 1948 ed.
  1. Holidays--Poetry. I. Clark, Robert Earle,
joint comp. II. Title.
PN6110.H4C63 1973   808.81'9'33   72-11861
ISBN 0-8369-6401-2

PRINTED IN THE UNITED STATES OF AMERICA

Acknowledgments

Acknowledgments

ACKNOWLEDGMENT is here made of the generous co-operation of both contributing poets and publishers in the making of this anthology. The compilers have made every effort to trace the ownership of all copyrighted poems. To the best of their knowledge they have secured all necessary permissions from authors or their authorized agents, or from both. If there has been any error regarding the use of any poem, the compilers will be pleased, upon notification of such error, to make proper acknowledgment in future editions of this book.

Sincere thanks are due the following publishers for co-operation in granting the use of poems by the authors indicated:

D. Appleton-Century Company: "Our Flag Forever" by Frank L. Stanton.

The Beacon Press: "O Beautiful, My Country" by Frederick L. Hosmer, from *Hymns of the Spirit*. By permission of The Beacon Press, Boston, Massachusetts, U.S.A.

Harper & Brothers: "Indifference" from *The Sorrows of God and Other Poems* by G. A. Studdert-Kennedy, copyright 1924 by Harper & Brothers. "The Lord of the World" from *I Believe* by G. A. Studdert-Kennedy, copyright 1921, 1930 by Harper & Brothers.

Henry Harrison, Poetry Publisher: "From Beyond" by Lucia Trent.

Houghton Mifflin Company: "On a Picture of Lincoln" by John Vance Cheney. "The Hand of Lincoln" by Edmund Clarence Stedman from *Stedman's Poetical Works*. "Lincoln" by John T. Trowbridge.

Charles Scribner's Sons: "Bethlehem Town," reprinted from *Sharps and Flats* by Eugene Field; copyright 1900, 1901, 1928 by Julia

Sutherland Field. "Star of the East," reprinted from *Songs and Other Verse* by Eugene Field; copyright 1896 by Charles Scribner's Sons, 1923 by Julia Sutherland Field. "America's Prosperity," reprinted from *The Red Flower* by Henry van Dyke; copyright 1917 by Charles Scribner's Sons, 1946 by Tertius van Dyke. "The Heart of the Tree," reprinted from *Poems* by Henry C. Bunner; copyright 1896 by Charles Scribner's Sons, 1923 by Alice L. Bunner. Used by permission of the publishers, Charles Scribner's Sons.

Thanks are due also to the *Christian Century*, which granted permission for the inclusion of many poems which appeared originally in its poetry columns.

Special acknowledgment is due the following poets, and heirs of poets, who gave personal permission that poems might be included in this anthology:

Emily Greene Balch for "The Flag Speaks."
Mary Dickerson Bangham for "Come, Holy Babe."
Janet Norris Bangs for "Design for Peace" from *Cornstalk Fiddle* published by the Decker Press.
Eleanor D. Breed for "Scapegoats."
William E. Brooks for "Inasmuch," "Memorial Day," and "Three Wise Kings."
Dorothy Burgess for "Earth Listens," "In His Steps," "Wild Weather," and "Youth" by her aunt, Katharine Lee Bates.
Gail Brook Burket for "Columbus Never Knew," "February 12, 1809," "House in Springfield," "Noel," and "Thought for a New Year."
Witter Bynner for "Prepare" and "The Day."
Ruth Ford Catlin for "Childlike Heart" by her sister, Ellen Weston Catlin.
Elizabeth Cheney for "There Is a Man on the Cross."
Karl M. Chworowsky for "Motherhood."
Leslie Savage Clark for "Beacon Light," "Litany for Peace," and "The Way."
Stanton A. Coblentz for "History of the Modern World" and "We Who Build Visions."
R. D. Comfort for "Make Way!" by Florence C. Comfort.
Vere Dargan for "City Trees."

Alta Booth Dunn for "Unknown Soldier."
Laura Bell Everett for "Resurgence" and "The Lament of the Voiceless."
Harold E. Fey for "We Who Are About to Die."
Mildred Fowler Field for "Carpenter Christ."
Natalie Flohr for "The Martyr."
Florence Kiper Frank for "Lincoln."
Ethel Romig Fuller for "Diary," "Fir Forest," "Mother—A Portrait," and "The Pioneer Mother."
Mae Winkler Goodman for "Memorial," "Washington," and "Your Glory, Lincoln."
Esther Lloyd Hagg for "His Garments" and "It Was Not Strange."
Molly Anderson Haley for "A Christmas Prayer," "And Lo, the Star!" "He Is Our Peace," and "We Have Seen His Star in the East."
Mary Hallet for "Calvary."
Ida S. Hines for "A Christmas Prayer" by Herbert H. Hines.
George E. Hoffman for "December 26" and "Victory Parade."
Maud Frazer Jackson for "New Years and Old."
J. M. Kilgour for "In Flanders Fields" by John McCrae.
Mary Eva Kitchel for "So Runs Our Song."
Raymond Kresensky for "Comrade, Remember."
Eunice Mitchell Lehmer for "Armistice."
Mary Sinton Leitch for "From Bethlehem Blown."
Elinor Lennen for "His Last Week," "Nor House nor Heart," "On Entering a Forest," "Pilgrimage," and "Praetorium Scene: Good Friday."
May Carleton Lord for "Prayer."
Lilith Lorraine for "If These Endure," "Let Dreamers Wake," and "Without Regret."
Adelaide Love for "Alchemy" and "No Sweeter Thing."
Ruphine A. McCarthy for "The Land Where Hate Should Die" by her husband, Denis A. McCarthy.
Arthur R. Mcdougall, Jr., for "Bitter Question," "It Isn't Far to Bethlehem," and "We Need a King."
Clyde McGee for "Mary at the Cross."
John G. Magee for "High Flight" by John Magee.
Virgil Markham for "A Prayer," "Brotherhood," "Conscripts of the Dream" (excerpt), "How Shall We Honor Them?" "Lincoln, the Man of the People" (excerpt), "Man-Making," "Peace," "The

6

Errand Imperious," "The New Trinity," and "The Toiler" (excerpt) by his father, Edwin Markham.

Margaret Nickerson Martin for "Judas Iscariot."

Juanita Miller for "Columbus" and "The Mothers of Men" by her father, Joaquin Miller.

John Richard Moreland for "A White Tree in Bloom," "Christ Is Crucified Anew," "If a Man Die," "O Years Unborn," "Only One King," "Song of Thanksgiving," "Symbols," and "The Splendid Lover."

Angela Morgan for "Let Us Declare" (excerpt).

Ida Norton Munson for "Assurance."

Meredith Nicholson for "From Bethlehem to Calvary."

G. Ashton Oldham for "America First!"

Erica Oxenham for "A Te Deum of the Commonplace" (excerpt), "For Beauty We Thank Thee," "Gratitude for Work," "The Goal and the Way," "The Valley of Decision," "We Thank Thee," and "Where Are You Going, Great-Heart?" by her father, John Oxenham.

Katharine B. Paine for "Danger" by her sister, Theodora L. Paine.

The Pennsylvania Company for "The New Mars" by Florence Earle Coates.

Robert B. Pettengill for "There Will Be Peace" by his wife, Margaret Miller Pettengill.

Edith Lovejoy Pierce for "Christmas Amnesty," "Great Powers Conference," and "Song of the Wise Men."

Jason Noble Pierce for "Which Sword?"

Chauncey R. Piety for "A New Patriotism," "Come Back, Lincoln," "Gifts," "Thanksliving," and "The Soul of Lincoln."

LeVan Roberts for "The Unemployed."

William R. Rockett, Sr., for "A Mother Before a Soldier's Monument" by his wife, Winnie Lynch Rockett.

E. Merrill Root for "Carpenter of Eternity."

Phoebe Smith for "Via Dolorosa."

Wendell Phillips Stafford for "Washington and Lincoln."

Arvel Steece for "There Is Yet Time" and "World Planners."

William L. Stidger for "I Saw God," "Motherhood," "The Cross and the Tree," "The Waste of War," and "We Are the Burden-Bearers" (excerpt).

Lucia Trent for "Architects of Dream," "Armistice Day," "Bread of Brotherhood," "It Is Not Too Late," "Mary's Son," "Song for Tomorrow," "The Dreamers Cry Their Dream," "These Are My

People," and "Toward a True Peace." Also for "Comrade Jesus,"
"No Armistice in Love's War," and "Toward a True Peace" by
Ralph Cheyney.
Helen Weber for "Lessons."
Claire Whitaker for "Easter," "My Country Is the World," "O
Mothers of the Human Race," and "The Starred Mother" by her
husband, Robert Whitaker.
B. Y. Williams for "Washington."

Contents

New Year's Day

THOUGHT FOR A NEW YEAR

Leave tarnished sorrow, disappointment, doubt,
    Old worry, prejudice, defeat and fear
Heaped like a cast-off weary load outside
    The shining portal of another year.

Untraveled hills and valleys gleam beyond
    That wayfarers attain with mounting zest.
Who bears no useless burden from the past
    Will find the miles ahead are always best.

                        —GAIL BROOK BURKET

FACING THE NEW YEAR

We pledge ourselves
To follow through the coming year
The light which God gives us:
The light of Truth, wherever it may lead;
The light of Freedom, revealing new opportunities for individual
    development and social service;
The light of Faith, opening new visions of the better world to be;
The light of Love, daily binding brother to brother and man to
    God in ever closer bonds of friendship and affection.
Guided by this light,
We shall go forward to the work of another year with steadfastness
    and confidence.

                        —AUTHOR UNKNOWN

From DIARY

The Old Year is a diary where is set
Down, page by dog-eared page, all that I knew
Of twelve months' joy, or sorrow, or regret;
A memo of the times when I was true
To trusts, to friends; what I have made of self.
Here violets are pressed . . . here is a blend
Of tears and ink . . . I'll place it on the shelf
When I have added these last words—"The End."

—ETHEL ROMIG FULLER

THE OLD YEAR

What is the Old Year? 'Tis a book
On which we backward sadly look,
Not willing quite to see it close,
For leaves of violet and rose
Within its heart are thickly strewn,
Marking love's dawn and golden noon;
And turned-down pages, noting days
Dimly recalled through memory's haze;
And tear-stained pages, too, that tell
Of starless nights and mournful knell
Of bells tolling through trouble's air
The De Profundis of despair—
The laugh, the tear, the shine, the shade,
All 'twixt the covers gently laid;
No uncut leaves; no page unscanned;
Close it and lay it in God's hand.

—CLARENCE URMY

THE OLD YEAR'S PRAYER

God of the seasons, hear my parting prayer,
  Faint on the frosty air:
Let the New Year take up the work I leave,
  And finish what I weave;
Give to the troubled nations lasting peace,
  The harvest's yield increase;
Help the bereaved their sorrows to endure,
  Care for the old and poor.

Bid him give patience to all those in pain,
  And to the parched fields rain;
Protect the fledgling in its little nest,
  See that the weary rest;
And when the midnight bells from tower and town
  Send their sweet message down,
Bring faith in God, a beacon in the night
  To guide mankind aright.

—MINNA IRVING

NEW YEARS AND OLD

Clear ringing of a bell
Beneath the midnight sky.
Some say, "It is a knell;
The Old Year has to die."
But years eternal are,
In thoughts and deeds that live.
The truth that was denied,
The sinning and the wrong,
The victories of love
And mercy's tender song—

13

To all the coming days
Will light and shadow give.
Old Years we cannot slay—
And would we, if we could?

No; memory is good,
Though eyes are wet with tears
For joys that are no more;
We gather from past years
So much of wisdom's store.
If we would not blindly grope
On the road that winds ahead,

Then experience and hope
Must ever with us tread,
And memory abide,
To warm the heart, and guide. . . .
Let thanks to God be said
That Old Years are not dead.

—MAUD FRAZER JACKSON

FAREWELL AND HAIL!

Old Year, going, take with you
All our failures, sorrows, too;
Memories of bitter years,
Old regrets and futile tears;
Fret and envy, greed and spite—
Take them with you, pray, tonight.
Pride too lofty, dreams too crude,
Hate, with all its venomed brood,
Discontent, our subtle foe—
Old Year, take them, as you go.

14

New Year, bright as dawning youth,
Bring us faith and love of truth,
Kindly thoughts of one and all,
Charity for those who fall,
Strength to help and zest to cheer,
Hope to banish doubt and fear.
Bring us quietness, content,
When your brimming months are spent.

Old Year, here is our farewell.
New Year, hail! We wish you well.

—THOMAS CURTIS CLARK

A NEW LEAF

He came to my desk with a quivering lip—
    The lesson was done.
"Dear Teacher, I want a new leaf," he said,
    "I have spoiled this one."
I took the old leaf, stained and blotted,
And gave him a new one all unspotted,
    And into his sad eyes smiled,
    "Do better, now, my child."

I went to the throne with a quivering soul—
    The Old Year was done.
"Dear Father, hast Thou a new leaf for me?
    I have spoiled this one."
He took the old leaf, stained and blotted,
And gave me a new one all unspotted,
    And into my sad heart smiled,
    "Do better, now, my child."

—KATHLEEN WHEELER

15

RING OUT, WILD BELLS

Ring out, wild bells, to the wild sky,
    The flying cloud, the frosty light:
    The year is dying in the night;
Ring out, wild bells, and let him die.

Ring out the old, ring in the new,
    Ring, happy bells, across the snow:
    The year is going, let him go;
Ring out the false, ring in the true.

Ring out the grief that saps the mind,
    For those that here we see no more;
    Ring out the feud of rich and poor,
Ring in redress to all mankind.

Ring out false pride in place and blood,
    The civic slander and the spite;
    Ring in the love of truth and right,
Ring in the common love of good.

Ring out old shapes of foul disease;
    Ring out the narrowing lust of gold;
    Ring out the thousand wars of old,
Ring in the thousand years of peace.

Ring in the valiant man and free,
    The larger heart, the kindlier hand;
    Ring out the darkness of the land,
Ring in the Christ that is to be.

                                —ALFRED TENNYSON

AT DAWN OF THE YEAR

Move on with a will, nor dream thou back
Though a light flashed out on the dead year's track;
Though the heart lies cold as a thing in its shroud—
There are hearts as stunned in the shifting crowd.
We move with the face toward a coming span;
We look not back where the deep seas ran!
There are lights to be struck through a darkened land.
With an onward tread and a strong right hand,
We dream again—aye, an onward dream;
We will burnish the days till they burn and gleam;
We will look not back where our light flashed out—
There are shuddering hearts we will dream about;
There are lights to be struck where hearts stand by some shroud;
We will strike if but one 'midst the shifting crowd.

—GEORGE KLINGLE

BELLS OF NEW YEAR

With great good cheer the bells ring out
    Upon the starry night;
No threat of war, no cries of hate
    Can thwart their loving might.
For all the sorrows of the year
    And all the dreams gone wrong
They would atone, and once again
    They flood the air with song.

They bring assurance of a day
    When joy shall come to earth;
They bid all hearts that now are sad
    To wait the world's rebirth—

17

A world in which good will shall reign,
In which all war shall cease.
Ring out, ye happy bells! Ring in
A bright new world of peace.

—ARTHUR GORDON FIELD

PRAYER

Bless Thou this year, O Lord!
Make rich its days
With health, and work, and prayer, and praise,
And helpful ministry
To needy folk.
Speak Thy soft word
In cloudy days;
Nor let us think ourselves forgot
When common lot
Of sorrow hems us round.
Let generous impulse shame the niggard dole
That dwarfs the soul.
May no one fail his share of work
Through selfish thought;
Each day fulfill Thy holy will
In yielded lives,
And still the tumult
Of desires
Debased.
May faith, and hope, and love,
Increase.
Bless Thou this year, O Lord!

—A. S. C. CLARKE

THE NEW YEAR

I am the New Year, and I come to you pure and unstained,
Fresh from the hand of God.
Each day, a precious pearl to you is given
That you must string upon the silver thread of Life;
Once strung, can never be unthreaded but stays
An undying record of your faith and skill.
Each golden, minute link you then must weld into the chain of
    hours
That is no stronger than its weakest link.
Into your hands is given all the wealth and power
To make your life just what you will.
I give to you, free and unstinted, twelve glorious months
Of soothing rain and sunshine golden;
The days for work and rest, the nights for peaceful slumber.
All that I have I give with love unspoken.
All that I ask—*you keep the faith unbroken!*

—J. D. TEMPLETON

THE MESSAGE OF THE BELLS

I looked upon the dreary waste
    Of man's ambition, lust and fear:
I judged all mortals in my haste—
    The New Year bells rang loud and clear!

I wept for all the wars of old,
    I doubted every dream of peace,
I sighed for mankind's lust of gold—
    The bells of New Year would not cease!

19

I saw the starving poor go down
Amid the battles of the strong;
I cursed the cruel, heartless town—
Again the bells burst into song!

They sang of peace, they sang good will,
They sang of love that soon must reign;
I mocked their song, but could not still
The flooding rapture of their strain.

And thus the bells ring on and on
In countless hearts that claim the Hope:
They hail the ever-coming dawn
Though all the nations darkly grope.

—THOMAS CURTIS CLARK

A NEW YEAR PRAYER

Father, I will not ask for wealth or fame,
Though once they would have joyed my carnal sense:
I shudder not to bear a hated name,
Wanting all wealth, myself my sole defense.
But give me, Lord, eyes to behold the truth;
A seeing sense that knows the eternal right;
A heart with pity filled, and gentlest ruth;
A manly faith that makes all darkness light:
Give me the power to labor for mankind;
Make me the mouth of such as cannot speak:
Eyes let me be to groping men, and blind;
A conscience to the base; and to the weak
Let me be hands and feet; and to the foolish, mind;
And lead still farther on such as Thy kingdom seek.

—THEODORE PARKER

RECONSECRATION

God of our lives, O hear our prayer
   As the New Year dawns and the Old Year goes.
Take from our hearts their load of care;
   Give to our souls Thine own repose
As we lay aside our fear and grief,
   Our countless failures, our spite and hate;
Give us Thy Spirit's sure relief
   As we our lives reconsecrate.

O bright New Year, may we take your lead
   Through the days to come with purpose true.
In life and thought, in word and deed,
   May we trust the best the long year through.
May every day bring us calm content—
   Knowing that God is ever near;
And when the precious months are spent
   May we greet with joy another year.

—DOROTHY GOULD

Lincoln's Birthday

FEBRUARY 12, 1809

Oh, setting sun, had you no aureole?
  And, winter stars, had you no song that night,
When leafless branches, clicking in the wind,
  Wrote shadow phrases in your frosty light?

Rough-timbered cabin in the wilderness,
  Had you no thought you sheltered from the cold
A child whose life would bless the lives of men
  Until humanity and earth grow old?

And, valiant mother of a newborn son,
  Had you no intimation of your fate?
Or did you cradle in your arms a child
  Which God and you were certain would be great?
                              —Gail Brook Burket

THE MASTERPIECE

A blend of mirth and sadness
  Of smiles and tears,
A quaint knight errant
  Of the pioneers;
A homely hero
  Of star and sod,
A peasant prince,
  A masterpiece of God.
                              —Walter Malone

22

From LINCOLN, THE MAN OF THE PEOPLE

The color of the ground was in him, the red earth,
The smack and tang of elemental things:
The rectitude and patience of the cliff,
The good-will of the rain that loves all leaves,
The friendly welcome of the wayside well,
The courage of the bird that dares the sea,
The gladness of the wind that shakes the corn,
The pity of the snow that hides all scars,
The secrecy of streams that make their way
Under the mountain to the rifted rock,
The tolerance and equity of light
That gives as freely to the shrinking flower
As to the great oak flaring to the wind—
To the grave's low hill as to the Matterhorn
That shoulders out the sky.

.   .   .   .

So came the Captain with the mighty heart;
And when the judgment thunders split the house,
Wrenching the rafters from their ancient rest,
He held the ridgepole up, and spiked again
The rafters of the Home. He held his place—
Held the long purpose like a growing tree—
Held on through blame and faltered not at praise—
Towering in calm roughhewn sublimity.
And when he fell in whirlwind, he went down
As when a lordly cedar, green with boughs,
Goes down with a great shout upon the hills,
And leaves a lonesome place against the sky.

—EDWIN MARKHAM

23

THE STAR OF SANGAMON

Not out of the East but the West
A Star and a Savior arose;
A light to an eager quest,
A spirit of grace possessed,
Of faith 'mid increasing woes,
Of wisdom manifest.
And, forth from the variant past
Of thraldom's darkness, at last
God's measureless love for man
Wrought through heredity's dower
The great American,
Whose soul was the perfect flower
Of patriot planting in soil
Kept moist by blood and tears,
And fertile by faithful toil
Throughout unnumbered years.

—LYMAN WHITNEY ALLEN

A MAN OF MEN

Bred in a low place, lord of little deeds,
He learned to rule his spirit, and he grew
Like the young oak with yearning for the sky.
Yet on his face was sadness, as if grief
Had chilled his singing childhood, ah, too soon,
Or love with her heart-summer came too late!
So with the world he wrestled for his life
And labored long in silence, his gaunt frame
Knotted with secret agonies; and so
Struggled through darkness upward till he stood
Rugged and resolute, a man of men!

—LEONARD CHARLES VAN NOPPEN

24

THE HAND OF LINCOLN

This was the hand that knew to swing
  The ax—since thus would Freedom train
Her son—and made the forest ring,
  And drove the wedge, and toiled amain.

Firm hand, that loftier office took,
  A conscious leader's will obeyed,
And, when men sought his word and look,
  With steadfast might the gathering swayed.

No courtier's, toying with a sword,
  Nor minstrel's, laid across a lute;
A chief's, uplifted to the Lord
  When all the kings of earth were mute!
                    —EDMUND CLARENCE STEDMAN

HOUSE IN SPRINGFIELD

Here in this simple house his presence clings
  To tranquil, sunlit rooms and quiet nooks,
About the silent hearth, and faded prints,
  The sturdy desk, and rocking chairs, and books.

He has not known the tomb upon the hill
  Where mortal dust reposes in long rest;
The formal grandeur of his distant shrine
  Could never seem so singularly blest.

For here alone we sense the man who crossed
  This portal and emerged into the ages:
The peer of all greathearted souls in earth's
  Most noble company of saints and sages.
                    —GAIL BROOK BURKET

25

ABRAHAM LINCOLN

This man whose homely face you look upon
Was one of Nature's masterful great men,
Born with strong arms that unfought victories won.
Direct of speech, and cunning with the pen,
Chosen for large designs, he had the art
Of winning with his humor, and he went
Straight to his mark, which was the human heart.
Wise, too, for what he could not break, he bent;
Upon his back, a more than Atlas load,
The burden of the Commonwealth was laid;
He stooped and rose up with it, though the road
Shot suddenly downwards, not a whit dismayed.
Hold, warriors, councilors, kings! All now give place
To this dead Benefactor of the Race.

—RICHARD HENRY STODDARD

A TRIBUTE

Lincoln, the man who freed the slave;
    Lincoln, whom never self enticed;
Slain Lincoln, worthy found to die
    A soldier of his Captain, Christ.

—AUTHOR UNKNOWN

THE MASTERFUL MAN

Lincoln arose! the masterful great man,
Girt with rude grandeur, quelling doubt and fear—
A more than king, yet in whose veins there ran
The red blood of the people, warm, sincere,
Blending of Puritan and Cavalier.

—HENRY TYRRELL

26

LINCOLN

He came not as the princes born to rule,
  But humbly, as the son of pioneers;
Like them, of stern necessity the tool,
  Heir to their solitude, their need, their tears.
Unschooled, unprepossessing, long unwanted
  By those he offered constantly to serve,
Ill-starred in love, in commerce, still undaunted
  He grew, though slighted, steadfast to deserve.
Little of grace or comeliness endearing,
  Nothing of wiles had he to smooth his way;
But strength, which first from deep woods wrenched his clearing,
  His birthright was, and sunlike brought his day.
And by its might a race stood forth unfettered,
A death-shocked nation lived, a world was bettered.

—CLYDE WALTON HILL

THE PEOPLE'S KING

Not oft such marvel the years reveal,
  Such beauteous thing,
  A People's King,
The chosen liege of a chosen weal,
  And Liberty's offering.

Not oft such product the fair world hath,
  A People's Own,
  On mightiest throne,
Whose strong foundations are Right and Faith,
  And virtue the cornerstone.

—LYMAN WHITNEY ALLEN

27

From THE COMMEMORATION ODE

Nature, they say, doth dote,
And cannot make a man
Save on some worn-out plan,
Repeating as by rote:
For him her Old World moulds aside she threw,
And, choosing sweet clay from the breast
Of the unexhausted West,
With stuff untainted shaped a hero new,
Wise, steadfast in the strength of God, and true.

. . . .

His was no lonely mountain peak of mind,
Thrusting to thin air o'er our cloudy bars,
A seamark now, now lost in vapors blind,
Broad prairie rather, genial, level-lined,
Fruitful and friendly for all human kind.

. . . .

Great captains, with their guns and drums,
Disturb our judgment for the hour,
But at last silence comes;
These are all gone, and, standing like a tower,
Our children shall behold his fame,
The kindly-earnest, brave, foreseeing man,
Sagacious, patient, dreading praise, not blame,
New birth of our new soil, the first American.
—JAMES RUSSELL LOWELL

ON A PICTURE OF LINCOLN

I read once more this care-worn, patient face,
And learn anew that sorrow is the dower
Of him that sinks himself to lift his race
Into the seat of peace and power.

How beautiful the homely features grow,
  How soft the light from out the mild, sad eyes,
The gleam from deeps of grief the soul must know
  To be so great—so kind, so wise!
                              —JOHN VANCE CHENEY

THE LINCOLN STATUE
(Gutzon Borglum, Sculptor)

A man who drew his strength from all,
  Because of all a part;
He led with wisdom, for he knew
  The common heart.

Its hopes, its fears his eye discerned,
  And, reading, he could share.
Its griefs were his, its burdens were
  For him to bear.

Its faith that wrong must sometime yield,
  That right is ever right,
Sustained him in the saddest hour,
  The darkest night.

In patient confidence he wrought,
  The people's will his guide,
Nor brought to his appointed task
  The touch of pride.

The people's man, familiar friend,
  Shown by the sculptor's art
As one who trusted, one who knew
  The common heart.
                              —W. F. COLLINS

29

AT THE LINCOLN TOMB [1]

This tomb, by loving hands up-piled
To him, the merciful and mild,
From age to age shall carry down
The glory of his great renown.

As the long centuries onward flow,
As generations come and go,
Wide and more wide his fame shall spread,
And greener laurels crown his head.

And when this pile is fallen to dust,
Its bronzes crumbled into rust,
Thy name, O Lincoln, still shall be
Revered and loved from sea to sea.

Lord of the Nations! grant us still
Another patriot sage, to fill
The seat of power, and save the State
From selfish greed. For this we wait.

—JOHN H. BRYANT

LINCOLN

Heroic soul, in homely garb half hid,
    Sincere, sagacious, melancholy, quaint;
What he endured, no less than what he did,
    Has reared his monument and crowned him saint.

—JOHN TOWNSEND TROWBRIDGE

[1] Part of a poem read by the author, brother of William Cullen Bryant, at the ceremonies in Springfield on the eighteenth anniversary of the death of Lincoln.

From THE EMANCIPATION GROUP

Let man be free! The mighty word
   He spake was not his own;
An impulse from the Highest stirred
   These chiselled lips alone.

The cloudy sign, the fiery guide,
   Along his pathway ran,
And Nature, through his voice, denied
   The ownership of man.

We rest in peace where these sad eyes
   Saw peril, strife, and pain;
His was the nation's sacrifice,
   And ours the priceless gain.
          —JOHN GREENLEAF WHITTIER

LINCOLN

What answer shall we make to them that seek
The living vision on a distant shore?
What words of life? The nations at our door
Believing, cry, "America shall speak!"
We are the strong to succor them, the weak,
We are the healers who shall health restore.
Dear God! Where our own tides of conflict pour,
Who shall be heard above the din and shriek!
Who, brothers? There was one stood undismayed
'Mid broil of battle and the rancorous strife,
Searching with pitiful eyes the souls of men.
Our martyr calls you, wants you! Now as then
The oppressed shall hear him and be not afraid;
And Lincoln dead shall lead you into life!
          —FLORENCE KIPER FRANK

COME BACK, LINCOLN

Come back, Lincoln,
  Come back, Lincoln,
Come back to old Kentucky
And set your people free.

Here in Harlan
  Coal-lords drive men,
Here in Harlan
  Coal-lords starve men,
    Women hunger,
    Children hunger,
Hear, O Lincoln, hear their crying!
Hear the coal-lords' guns replying!

Come back, Lincoln,
Come back to old Kentucky
And set your people free.

—CHAUNCEY R. PIETY

"THOU SHOULDST BE LIVING AT THIS HOUR!"

Lincoln! "Thou shouldst be living at this hour!"
Thy reach of vision—prophet thou and seer—
Thy strong and steadfast wisdom, judgment clear,
Are needed in this stress, thy oldtime power
The ship of state to save from storms that lower
And threaten to engulf. Dark reefs loom near.
No "watchful waiting" will avail us here,
Our wind-swept, tossing ship past rocks that tower
To guide to sunlit waters—calm, serene.
Oh! for a leader, fearless, strong and wise,

Of swift decision, and with insight keen
To see the dangers; scorn all compromise;
Restore the honor lost, the faith we prize,
And bring us back the glory that hath been!

—KENYON WEST

LINCOLN, COME BACK

Lincoln, come back, rebuke us for our sins—
The sin of greed, of blatant pride and hate.
Our earth goes blindly to a hopeless fate
Unless for us a new, kind world begins.
Renew our dreams—who dreamed a world made free;
Give us new hope for world-wide liberty.
Lincoln, come back, rebuke us for our sins.

Lincoln, come back, once more our prophet be.
Lead forth the nations in a pact of peace;
Teach us that selfishness and greed must cease
That men may dwell in love and harmony.
Your kindly heart—that it might plan our weal!
Your mighty hand—how powerful to heal!
Lincoln, come back, once more our prophet be.

Lincoln, come back, rebuild our broken world.
Shattered and torn, the nations face the night;
Earth's leaders halt, bereft of vision's light;
Humanity's fair banner now is furled;
The surging peoples now are leaderless;
They ask a friend, and there is none to bless.
Lincoln, come back, rebuild our broken world.

—THOMAS CURTIS CLARK

THE SOUL OF LINCOLN

"Now, he belongs to the ages";
  Yes, Stanton, your dictum is true—
Lives with the seers and the sages
  Who fashion the nation anew.

Dubbing him "homely old dreamer,"
  They plotted and thrust him aside;
Dead is the scheme and the schemer,
  But Abe and his dreams will abide.

Flesh ill-became the immortal,
  And neither could flesh understand;
Now he returns from the portal
  Of death with a mightier hand.

Flesh is as nothing to spirit,
  No state and no land can confine;
Earth is enlarged to inherit
  The soul of your Lincoln and mine.
                    —CHAUNCEY R. PIETY

HIS LIVING MONUMENT

Though many a year above his dust
  Has shed its suns and rains,
A pattern still for all the world
  His memory remains.
And laurel wreath and martyr's crown
  Around his name are blent,
And every black he freed is now
  His living monument.
                    —MINNA IRVING

34

LINCOLN'S BIRTHDAY

A sacred day is this,
　A day to bless;
A day that leads to bliss
　Through bitterness.
For on this day of days,
　One wondrous morn,
In far off forest ways
　Was Lincoln born.

Who supped the cup of tears,
　Who ate the bread
Of sorrow and of fears,
　Of war and dread;
Yet from this feast of woes,
　His people's pride,
A loved immortal rose
　All glorified!

　　　　　—JOHN KENDRICK BANGS

YOUR GLORY, LINCOLN

No myrtle can obliterate a name
Carved not on stone, but in a Nation's heart;
This is your glory, Lincoln, and your fame—
None will forget how you rehearsed your part
(Oh, did you know, oh did you even then
Know that was but the prologue to the play?
That brother would slay brother soon again
Upon a vaster stage . . . a later day?)

35

A house divided cannot stand, you said;
You knew that slavery held the master slave—
That freedom is man's sustenance and bread;
Your voice still pleads beneath the vaulted grave. . . .
You cannot sleep till man has understood
That peace is Universal Brotherhood!

—MAE WINKLER GOODMAN

THE GLORY OF LINCOLN

Who builds of stone a shrine to bear his name,
    Shall be forgot when months and years have flown;
Who writes his name upon the scroll of fame,
    The centuries shall find to men unknown;
But who for fellow men endured the shame
    Shall have eternal glory for his own.

—THOMAS CURTIS CLARK

Washington's Birthday

WASHINGTON AND LINCOLN

Two stars alone of primal magnitude,
Twin beacons in our firmament of fame,
Shine for all men with benison the same:
On day's loud labor by the night renewed,
On templed silences where none intrude,
On leaders followed by the street's acclaim,
The solitary student by his flame,
The watcher in the battle's interlude.
All ways and works of men they shine upon;
And now and then beneath their golden light
A sudden meteor reddens and is gone;
And now and then a star grows strangely bright,
Drawing all eyes, then dwindles on the night;
And the eternal sentinels shine on.

—WENDELL PHILLIPS STAFFORD

[WHOM WE REVERE]
From UNDER THE OLD ELM

Haughty they said he was, at first, severe;
But owned, as all men own, the steady hand
Upon the bridle, patient to command,
Prized, as all prize, the justice pure from fear,
And learned to honor first, then love him, then revere.

—JAMES RUSSELL LOWELL

WASHINGTON

Long are the years since he fell asleep
  Where the Potomac flows gently by,
There where Mount Vernon's green stretches sweep
  Under the blue Virginia sky.
Warrior and statesman and patriot true,
  Well had he wielded both sword and pen.
Truly, they said as they laid him to rest,
  "First in the hearts of his countrymen."
Long are the years—and the land he loved
  Stands among nations, grown strong and great;
True to his vision of long ago,
  Proud of the hand that so shaped her fate.
Time but adds splendor to fame so fair,
  Years but test greatness—and now as then
Sleeps he in peace on Mount Vernon's hill,
  "First in the hearts of his countrymen."
                              —B. Y. WILLIAMS

[IMPERIAL MAN]
From UNDER THE OLD ELM

Virginia gave us this imperial man
Cast in the massive mould
Of those high-statured ages old
Which into grander forms our mortal metal ran;
She gave us this unblemished gentleman:
What shall we give her back but love and praise
As in the dear old unestrangèd days
Before the inevitable wrong began?
Mother of States and undiminished men,
Thou gavest us a country, giving him,
And we owe alway what we owed thee then.
                      —JAMES RUSSELL LOWELL

38

AT MOUNT VERNON

Along this path he walked, great Washington,
Who built a nation out of selfish men;
These trees he planted, here he stood and mused
On spring's first blossoms, or on autumn's gain.
By this loved river, flowing wide and free,
He sighed for rest from all the cares of state.
How dear his home! And yet he could not pause
While traitors tore his land with greed and hate;
He could not free himself, whose character
Was part and parcel of his country's name.
He found no lasting rest, though worn and spent,
Till death relieved him from the bonds of fame.
Through all the years, till freedom's day is run,
One name shall shine with splendor—WASHINGTON.
　　　　　　　　　　　—THOMAS CURTIS CLARK

[THE GREAT VIRGINIAN]
From UNDER THE OLD ELM

Never to see a nation born
Hath been given to mortal man,
Unless to those who, on that summer morn,
Gazed silent when the great Virginian
Unsheathed the sword whose fatal flash
Shot union through the incoherent clash
Of our loose atoms, crystallizing them
Around a single will's unpliant stem,
And making purpose of emotions rash.
Out of that scabbard sprang, as from its womb,
Nebulous at first but hardening to a star,
Through mutual share of sunburst and of gloom,
The common faith that makes us what we are.
　　　　　　　　　　　—JAMES RUSSELL LOWELL

THE NAME OF WASHINGTON

America, the land beloved,
  Today reveres the name of him
Whose character was free from guile,
  Whose fame the ages cannot dim.

They called him proud, but erred therein;
  No lord was he, though high of birth;
Though sprung from England's lofty peers,
  He served the lowliest of earth.

He turned his back on pride of name,
  On motherland and luxury,
To weld a horde of quarreling men
  Into a nation proudly free.

Wherever liberty is found,
  Wherever shines fair freedom's sun,
Men count America a friend
  And bless the name of Washington.
      —ARTHUR GORDON FIELD

WHEN SHALL WE SEE THY LIKE AGAIN?

O noble brow, so wise in thought!
O heart so true! O soul unbought!
O eye so keen to pierce the night,
And guide the ship of state aright!

O life so simple, grand and free;
The humblest still may turn to thee.
O king uncrowned! O prince of men!
When shall we see thy like again?
      —MARY WINGATE

WASHINGTON'S PRAYER FOR THE NATION

May we unite in most humbly offering our prayers and supplications
To the Great Lord and Ruler of Nations,
And to beseech Him to pardon our national and other transgressions;
To enable us all, whether in public or private stations,
To perform our several and relative duties properly and punctually;
To render our national government a blessing to all the people
By constantly being a government of wise, just and constitutional laws,
Discreetly and faithfully executed and obeyed;
To protect and guide all sovereigns and nations,
And to bless them with good governments, peace and concord;
To promote the knowledge and practice of true religion and virtue,
And, generally, to grant unto all mankind such a degree of temporal prosperity
As He alone knows to be best.

—GEORGE WASHINGTON

INSCRIPTION AT MOUNT VERNON

Washington, the brave, the wise, the good,
Supreme in war, in council, and in peace.
Valiant without ambition, discreet without fear, confident without assumption.
In disaster calm; in success moderate; in all, himself.
The hero, the patriot, the Christian.
The father of nations, the friend of mankind,
Who, when he had won all, renounced all, and sought in the bosom of his family and of nature, retirement, and in the hope of religion, immortality.

41

HIS TASK—AND OURS

August, revered,
  Our nation's sire,
By years of toil,
  Through battles dire,
You bought for us
  Our far-flung land,
A home for freemen
  Dreamed and planned.

God grant that we
  Who praise your name
And priceless worth,
  Who hail your fame,
Shall through the years,
  Undaunted, plan
To make the world
  A Home for Man.

—DOROTHY GOULD

WASHINGTON

Another year has struck the vibrant chime
And still you sleep; roots stir beneath the tomb,
And yet you do not know, immune to time,
Beyond the reach of spring's returning bloom;
Yet still, at times, our love, O Washington,
Must penetrate the very walls of breath;
A father surely hears a loving son
Beyond the barrier of time ... and death.

42

And so we speak again; perhaps you hear
The echo of an echo, and you know
How through the fateful years you grow more dear,
Your name a symbol; be it ever so.
Now, more than ever, in our time of need,
We turn for strength and comfort to thy creed.
—MAE WINKLER GOODMAN

FIRST CITIZEN

His work well done, the leader stepped aside,
Spurning a crown with more than kingly pride,
Content to wear the higher crown of worth,
While time endures, First Citizen of earth.
—JAMES JEFFREY ROCHE

[OURS, AND ALL MEN'S]
From UNDER THE OLD ELM

Soldier and statesman, rarest unison;
High-poised example of great duties done
Simply as breathing, a world's honors worn
As life's indifferent gifts to all men born;
Dumb for himself, unless it were to God,
But for his barefoot soldier eloquent,
Tramping the snow to coral where they trod,
Held by his awe in hollow-eyed content;
Modest, yet firm as Nature's self; unblamed
Save by the men his nobler temper shamed;

. . . .

Not honored then or now because he wooed
The popular voice, but that he still withstood;
Broadminded, higher-souled, there is but one
Who was all this and ours, and all men's—WASHINGTON.
—JAMES RUSSELL LOWELL

Lent and Easter

FROM BETHLEHEM TO CALVARY

From Bethlehem to Calvary the Savior's journey lay;
Doubt, unbelief, scorn, fear and hate beset Him day by day,
But in His heart He bore God's love that brightened all the way.

O'er the Judean hills He walked, serene and brave of soul,
Seeking the beaten paths of men, touching and making whole,
Dying at last for love of man, on Calvary's darkened knoll.

He went with patient step and slow, as one who scatters seed;
Like a fierce hunger in His heart He felt the world's great need,
And the negations Moses gave He changed to loving deed.

From Bethlehem to Calvary the world still follows on,
Even as the halt and blind of old along His path were drawn;
Through Calvary's clouds they seek the light that led Him to the
dawn.

—MEREDITH NICHOLSON

FOR OUR SAKES

O smitten mouth! O forehead crowned with thorn!
    O Chalice of all common miseries!
Thou for our sakes that loved Thee not hast borne
    An agony of endless centuries,
And we were vain and ignorant nor knew
That when we stabbed Thy heart it was our own real hearts we
    slew.

—OSCAR WILDE

44

"THE WAY"

So short the road from Bethlehem
   That led to Calvary,
So thronged with halt and maimed and blind,
   Beggar and Pharisee.

So dark the slope of that last hill.
   Yet up that way He trod
Man follows over the centuries—
   Home to the heart of God!
                —LESLIE SAVAGE CLARK

CALVARY AND EASTER

A song of sunshine through the rain,
   Of spring across the snow;
A balm to heal the hurts of pain,
   A peace surpassing woe.
Lift up your heads, ye sorrowing ones,
   And be ye glad of heart,
For Calvary and Easter Day
   Were just three days apart!

With shudder of despair and loss
   The world's deep heart is wrung, .
As, lifted high upon his cross,
   The Lord of Glory hung—
When rocks were rent, and ghostly forms
   Stole forth in street and mart;
But Calvary and Easter Day,
Earth's blackest day, and whitest day,
   Were just three days apart.
                —AUTHOR UNKNOWN

45

GOOD FRIDAY IN MY HEART

Good Friday in my heart! Fear and affright!
My thoughts are the Disciples when they fled,
My words the words that priest and soldier said,
My deed the spear to desecrate the dead.
And day, Thy death therein, is changed to night.

Then Easter in my heart sends up the sun.
My thoughts are Mary, when she turned to see.
My words are Peter, answering, "Lov'st thou Me?"
My deeds are all Thine own drawn close to Thee,
And night and day, since Thou dost rise, are one.

—MARY ELIZABETH COLERIDGE

THE MARTYR

And all the while they mocked him and reviled,
And heaped upon him words of infamy,
He stood serenely there, and only smiled
In pity at the blind intensity
Of hate; for well he knew that Love alone
Can cure the ills of men—of nations, too—
Though unregenerate mobs their prophets stone,
And crucify the gentle Christ anew.
So he but smiled, and drained with quiet grace
The bitter cup for lips too eloquent,
And, dauntless, took the soul-degrading place
Designed for thieves—this Prophet heaven-sent!
And when the throng at length had hushed its cry,
Another cross loomed dark against the sky.

—NATALIE FLOHR

46

HIS GARMENTS

He gave his life upon the cross;
  To those who hung him there
He gave forgiveness—and he left
  His clothes for them to wear!

That seamless vesture from whose hem
  Heaven's healing power stole,
Was worn above a Roman heart!
  Oh, was that heart made whole?

Each hand that smote the thorn-crowned head,
  Each arm that drove a nail,
He covered with his raiment fair,
  And blood drops for them fell.

Was it I who pierced Thy side, my God,
  And looked upon Thee there?
White garments from Thy stainless life
  Oh, give me, Lord, to wear!
                    —Esther Lloyd Hagg

CRUCIFIXION

Golgotha's journey is an ancient way
  That leads from Rome's outrageous judgment gate
To modern slums and trenches, where we pray
  To him whose heart is breaking with our hate.

We build his crosses now of steel and lead,
  And pierce his body with the bayonet;
Behind the trenches watch his blood flow red
  In flaming anguish that we soon forget.

47

Lord Caesar's high tribunal, Martian-wise,
 Spits in his face—Rome never was more rude!—
And in the name of freedom still denies
 To Christian men the right of rectitude.

For greed and self-enthronement are the same,
 And Jesus bleeds in every clan and clime;
All down the ages with its lashing shame
 He bears the insult—Love his only crime.

—Hugh O. Isbell

INDIFFERENCE

When Jesus came to Golgotha they hanged Him on a tree,
They drave great nails through hands and feet, and made a Calvary;
They crowned Him with a crown of thorns, red were His wounds and deep,
For those were crude and cruel days, and human flesh was cheap.

When Jesus came to Birmingham they simply passed Him by,
They never hurt a hair of Him, they only let Him die;
For men had grown more tender, and they would not give Him pain,
They only just passed down the street, and left Him in the rain.

Still Jesus cried, "Forgive them, for they know not what they do,"
And still it rained the wintry rain that drenched Him through and through;
The crowds went home and left the streets without a soul to see,
And Jesus crouched against a wall and cried for Calvary.

—G. A. Studdert-Kennedy

SYMBOLS

I never see upon a hill
  Cedar or pine or olive tree,
But what I think of One who died
  On Calvary.

I never hear the hammer's ring
  Driving the nail deep in the wood,
But that I see pale hands whose palms
  Are red with blood.

I never feel the dark come down
  But that I hear a piercing cry
That tears my heart. "Eloi . . . lama
  Sabachthani!"

        —JOHN RICHARD MORELAND

CARPENTER OF ETERNITY

A carpenter, he worked with wood—
  The fragrant wood and pale:
He planed the broad and feathery coils
  And drove the drastic nail.

And from the cedar and the oak—
  The texture of the tree—
He built the House of Time before
  That of Eternity.

How strange to choose a carpenter
  And bind him and impale
Upon the wood he used to work—
  With the beloved nail!

        —E. MERRILL ROOT

49

SO RUNS OUR SONG

A dozen sandaled saints I see
Walk the sad soil of Galilee.

Right loud I laud the humble land,
    And the holy crop she grew.
Yet how I love my leech-fed Rome—
    Her tubs and temples, too.
I'd die the death before I'd be
A sandaled saint of Galilee.

So runs our song. And you and I
The Shining One still crucify,
Spit in his face, and pass him by.

                    —MARY EVA KITCHEL

I SAW GOD

I saw God bare his soul one day
    Where all the earth might see
The stark and naked heart of him
    On lonely Calvary.

There was a crimson sky of blood
    And overhead a storm;
When lightning slit the clouds
    And light engulfed his form.

Beyond the storm a rainbow lent
    A light to every clod,
And on that cross mine eyes beheld
    The naked soul of God.

                    —WILLIAM L. STIDGER

50

WEDNESDAY IN HOLY WEEK

Man's life is death. Yet Christ endured to live,
  Preaching and teaching, toiling to and fro,
Few men accepting what He yearned to give,
  Few men with eyes to know
  His Face, that Face of Love He stooped to show.

Man's death is life. For Christ endured to die
  In slow unuttered weariness of pain,
A curse and an astonishment, passed by,
  Pointed at, mocked again
  By men for whom He shed His Blood—in vain?
                              —CHRISTINA ROSSETTI

THUS SPEAKETH CHRIST OUR LORD[1]

Ye call Me Master and obey Me not,
Ye call Me Light and see Me not,
Ye call Me Way and walk Me not,
Ye call Me Life and desire Me not,
Ye call Me wise and follow Me not,
Ye call Me fair and love Me not,
Ye call Me rich and ask Me not,
Ye call Me eternal and seek Me not,
Ye call Me gracious and trust Me not,
Ye call Me noble and serve Me not,
Ye call Me mighty and honor Me not,
Ye call Me just and fear Me not;
If I condemn you, blame Me not.
                              —AUTHOR UNKNOWN

[1] Engraved on a slab in the Cathedral of Lübeck in Germany.

51

PRAETORIUM SCENE: GOOD FRIDAY

Rome did its worst; thorns platted for his brow,
    Face spat upon, with sneers and venomed curse,
His body beaten; reason questions how
    Malicious men could make his suffering worse.

But after flesh and blood could bear no more,
    His mind must suffer this indignity:
The scarlet robe the military wore
    Put on the Prince of Peace, for mockery!
                    —ELINOR LENNEN

THERE IS A MAN ON THE CROSS

Whenever there is silence around me
By day or by night—
I am startled by a cry.
It came down from the cross—
The first time I heard it.
I went out and searched—
And found a man in the throes of crucifixion,
And I said, "I will take you down,"
And I tried to take the nails out of his feet.
But he said, "Let them be,
For I cannot be taken down
Until every man, every woman, and every child
Come together to take me down."
And I said, "But I cannot bear your cry.
What can I do?"
And he said, "Go about the world—
Tell every one that you meet—
There is a man on the cross."
                    —ELIZABETH CHENEY

52

INASMUCH!

I saw the Lord Christ tonight,
  Walking the streets of my town,
With hair blown wild with the winter wind,
  With the wild rain beating down.

"I am hungry and bitter cold,
  Hungry and cold," he said.
"What?" I cried, "have your folk denied
  Shelter to you, and bread?"

"What is hunger to Me,
  And what is the lashing rain,
Who died on a Tree on Calvary,
  Sharing the ultimate pain?

"But the folk in the fetid slum,
  Neglected in alleys old,
These go unfed with the living Bread,
  Blue with a starved soul's cold.

"So I walk the streets in pain,
  More pain than I knew on the Tree;
Inasmuch as ye did it not to them
  Ye did it not to Me."

—WILLIAM E. BROOKS

DYING

Beauty goes out to meet a greater beauty,
  Something we cannot grasp, who cry our loss—
Something God meant when he made the first morning,
  Something *he* meant, who stumbled with a cross!

—JESSIE HOLT

53

COMRADE JESUS

I tramped the pavements, cursing God,
When there beside me Jesus trod!

Now we shall walk, my Friend and I,
Across the earth, the sea, the sky.

I do not know what he may be;
I only know he walks with me.

From Eden barred and Paradise,
Too wisely sad, too sadly wise!

Oh, lonely feet! Oh, bleeding feet!
In step with mine on the city street!

—RALPH CHEYNEY

ONLY ONE KING

In arrogance and vanity
Kings sculpture regal words and creeds
On granite, that posterity
May marvel at their mighty deeds
Of war and conquest; time and rust
Grind these memorials to dust.

Only one King came scorning power,
Walked with the humble of the land
And served mankind his willing hour:
And he wrote only on the sand!

—JOHN RICHARD MORELAND

STILL THOU ART QUESTION

We place Thy sacred name upon our brows;
  Our cycles from Thy natal day we score:
Yet, in spite of all our songs and all our vows,
  We thirst and ever thirst to know Thee more.

For Thou art Mystery and Question still;
  Even when we see Thee lifted as a sign
Drawing all men unto that hapless hill
  With the resistless power of love divine.

Still Thou art Question—while rings in our ears
  Thine outcry to a world discord-beset:
Have I been with thee all these many years,
  O World—dost thou not know Me even yet?
                              —AUTHOR UNKNOWN

FOLLOW ME

And Him evermore I beheld
  Walking in Galilee;
Through the cornfield's waving gold,
In hamlet, in wood, in wold,
  By the shores of the Beautiful Sea.
He toucheth the sightless eyes,
  Before Him the demons flee;
To the dead He sayeth, "Arise!"
  To the living, "Follow me!"
And that voice shall still sound on
From the centuries that are gone
  To the centuries that shall be.
                    —HENRY WADSWORTH LONGFELLOW

From THE HEALER

So stood the holy Christ
  Amidst the suffering throng;
With whom his lightest touch sufficed
  To make the weakest strong.

That healing gift he lends to them
  Who use it in his name;
The power that filled his garment's hem
  Is evermore the same.

That Good Physician liveth yet
  Thy friend and guide to be;
The Healer by Gennesaret
  Shall walk the rounds with thee.

—JOHN GREENLEAF WHITTIER

PRAYER OF A MODERN THOMAS

If Thou, O God, the Christ didst leave,
In him, not Thee, I do believe;
  To Jesus dying, all alone,
  To his dark Cross, not Thy bright Throne,
My hopeless hands will cleave.

But if it was Thy love that died,
Thy voice that in the darkness cried,
  The print of nails I long to see,
  In Thy hands, God, who fashioned me,
Show me Thy piercèd side.

—EDWARD SHILLITO

56

CALVARY

A dying figure against the sky;
Laughter mocking a piteous cry;
Terror, silence, an anguished plea:
"Father, forgive them, they do not see!"

Piercing the darkness like singing flame,
"My Love shall enfold them!" the answer came.
—MARY HALLET

CHRIST IS CRUCIFIED ANEW

Not only once, and long ago,
There on Golgotha's rugged side,
Has Christ, the Lord, been crucified
Because He loved a lost world so.
But hourly souls, sin-satisfied,
Mock His great love, flout His commands.
And I drive nails deep in His hands,
You thrust the spear within His side.
—JOHN RICHARD MORELAND

THE MAN OF SORROWS

Christ claims our help in many a strange disguise;
Now, fever-ridden, on a bed he lies;
Homeless he wanders now beneath the stars;
Now counts the number of his prison bars;
Now bends beside us, crowned with hoary hairs.
No need have we to climb the heavenly stairs,
And press our kisses on his feet and hands;
In every man that suffers, he, the Man of Sorrows, stands!
—AUTHOR UNKNOWN

57

QUATRAIN

Christ bears a thousand crosses now
　　Where once but one he bore;
Each cruel deed unto his brow
　　Adds one thorn more.

　　　　　　　　　　—CHARLES G. BLANDEN

GIFTS

Christ gave a yoke, a sword, a cross,
　　And men gave him disdain;
Fools took the gifts, dared pain and loss,
　　And the world is their domain.

　　　　　　　　　　—CHAUNCEY R. PIETY

STILL AS OF OLD

Still as of old
　　Men by themselves are priced—
For thirty pieces Judas sold
　　Himself, not Christ.

　　　　　　　　　　—HESTER H. CHOLMONDELEY

IN HIS STEPS

Should not the glowing lilies of the field
　　With keener splendor mark his footsteps yet—
Prints of the gentle feet whose passing healed
　　All blight from Tabor unto Olivet?

　　　　　　　　　　—KATHARINE LEE BATES

GOOD FRIDAY EVENING

No Cherub's heart or hand for us might ache,
   No Seraph's heart of fire had half sufficed;
Thine own were pierced and broken for our sake,
   O Jesus Christ.

Therefore we love Thee with our faint good will,
   We crave to love Thee not as heretofore,
To love Thee much, to love Thee more and still
   More and yet more.

—CHRISTINA ROSSETTI

WE NEED A KING

We need a King!
A Man to wake our dreams;
For all the world is sick at heart
With screaming down the priests of Baal,
Who hold at least the greater part.

We need a King!
Not born among our rich,
For they have lost the tender mind;
Not nursed by noisy women, nor
Of those who weep, and yet are blind.

We need a King
With scars upon his hands;
But if one comes to take the throne,
I will demand to see his side
Before I make this King my own.

—ARTHUR R. MACDOUGALL, JR.

ASSURANCE

Full many are the centuries since the days
When early Christians traveled to great shrines,
Weary and spent, along hot, dusty ways,
To hear, at Easter time, the blessed lines
Read to assure them of the living Christ—
Words that could strengthen faith, sorrow allay.
These pilgrims counted it a thing unpriced
To hear again, "The stone was rolled away."

No distant journey needs must be to feel
The joy that pulses with new bud and leaf;
And here, in Easter quiet, heart may kneel
To grasp his comfort after winter grief.
As Mary, weeping, found her doubt had fled,
I, too, know "Christ is risen, as he said."

—IDA NORTON MUNSON

JESUS LIVES!

Jesus lives! thy terrors now
   Can no longer, death, appall us;
Jesus lives! by this we know
   Thou, O grave, canst not enthrall us.
       Hallelujah!

Jesus lives! henceforth is death
   But the gate to life immortal;
This shall calm our trembling breath
   When we pass its gloomy portal.
       Hallelujah!

—C. F. GELLERT

EASTER CAROL

O Earth, throughout thy borders
  Re-don thy fairest dress;
And everywhere, O Nature,
  Throb with new happiness!
Once more to new creation
  Awake, and death gainsay,
For death is swallowed up of life,
  And Christ is risen today.

Let peals of jubilation
  Ring out in all the lands;
With hearts of deep elation
  Let sea with sea clasp hands;
Let one supreme Te Deum
  Roll round the world's highway,
For death is swallowed up of life,
  And Christ is risen today.

—George Newell Lovejoy

BEACON LIGHT

Whenever I come on kelp-stained nets
  Drying along the sands,
I think of four bronzed fishermen,
  And my heart understands
How joyfully they laid aside
  Their nets by Galilee
To follow one clear Beacon Light
  Across eternity.

—Leslie Savage Clark

JUDAS ISCARIOT

Judas was I! Ah, the mockery!
  For I thought he could not die.
What did the silver mean to me
  When I heard my Master's cry?

If I had known that he understood;
  Forgave me! Aye, and blessed!
Would I have taken the coward's way
  If I had known or guessed?

Greater my grief than heart could bear
  After the fear and doubt;
What was left in the world for me
  After the Light was out?

—MARGARET NICKERSON MARTIN

HIS LAST WEEK

Sunday, the shout of hosannas,
The triumph of palms in Jerusalem.

Friday, the cross on Golgotha,
The mocking of thorns in a diadem.

Highest to lowest, in only a five days' span;
Hailed Son of God, and made the derision of man.

Sunday again, and the grave, and the seal strangely
  broken,
And those who had doubted remembering words
  he had spoken.

—ELINOR LENNEN

62

THE SPLENDID LOVER

One and one only
Is the splendid lover,
The all-forgiving,
All-compassionate;
When others fret you
With impatient loving,
He, a greater lover,
Patiently will wait.

Though you turn from him
Threescore years and seven,
Mock his devotion,
Spurn him as a guest,
With unceasing ardor
He, at last, will win you,
And reveal love's wonder
When your head lies on his breast.

—JOHN RICHARD MORELAND

RESURRECTION

The day of resurrection,
    Earth, tell it out abroad,
The Passover of gladness,
    The Passover of God.
From death to life eternal,
    From earth unto the sky,
Our Christ hath brought us over
    With hymns of victory.

—JOHN OF DAMASCUS

"IF A MAN DIE—"

I will repudiate the lie
Men tell of life;
How it will pass
As fragile flower or butterfly.
Whose dust shall nourish
April grass.

Since One, for love, died on a tree
And in the stony
Tomb was laid,
Behold I show a mystery:
All sepulchers
Are sealed in vain!

—John Richard Moreland

IF EASTER BE NOT TRUE

If Easter be not true,
Then all the lilies low must lie;
The Flanders poppies fade and die;
The spring must lose her fairest bloom
For Christ were still within the tomb—
If Easter be not true.

If Easter be not true,
Then faith must mount on broken wing;
Then hope no more immortal spring;
Then hope must lose her mighty urge;
Life prove a phantom, death a dirge—
If Easter be not true.

64

If Easter be not true,
'Twere foolishness the cross to bear;
He died in vain who suffered there;
What matter though we laugh or cry,
Be good or evil, live or die,
    If Easter be not true?

If Easter be not true—
But it is true, and Christ is risen!
And mortal spirit from its prison
Of sin and death with him may rise!
Worthwhile the struggle, sure the prize,
    Since Easter, aye, is true!

—HENRY H. BARSTOW

EASTER

With song and sun-burst comes the Easter morn:
Yet was there sunset ere the sun arose;
Under the sod, the rain-drift and the snows,
The nurturing of life, wherefrom was born
The blossom on the breast of beauty worn?
Each way of glory through some garden goes
Where midnight yet a deeper midnight knows,
Against the halo, cross and scourge and thorn.
Will it be always so? the Easter still
Always the answer to what seemeth ill?
Or shall we some day know that all is good
If but the all, at last, be understood?
This the consummate Easter that shall be
In the full sun-burst of Eternity!

—ROBERT WHITAKER

WHAT DOES EASTER MEAN TO YOU?

What does Easter mean to you?
Stately church with cushioned pew,
Where, Lenten season gone at last
And days of self-denial past,
Richly-clad, devoted throngs
Of worshipers unite in songs
Of praise in lily-scented air?
Is this what makes your Easter fair?

Does it mean the end of winter's reign,
Bright skies and welcome warmth again,
Singing of birds, budding of trees,
Sweet spring odors on the breeze
From daffodil and crocus bed
And balsam branches overhead?
Sad is the world and cold and gray,
If this is all of Easter Day.

But if this blessèd season brings
A firmer faith in holy things;
Assurance of a living Lord;
A strengthening of the tender chord
Of love that binds us to the life to come
Where loved ones 'wait us in the heavenly home,
No pain or loss can e'er efface the bliss,
Dear friend, of Easter when it means all this.

—MAY RICKER CONRAD

EASTER DAY

Weep not beside his tomb,
Ye women unto whom
He was great comfort and yet greater grief;
Nor ye, ye faithful few that wont with him to roam,
Seek sadly what for him ye left, go hopeless to your home;
Nor ye despair, ye sharers yet to be of their belief;
   Though he be dead, he is not dead,
   Nor gone, though fled,
   Not lost, though vanishèd;
   Though he return not, though
   He lies and molders low;
   In the true creed
   He is yet risen indeed;
    Christ is yet risen.
      —ARTHUR HUGH CLOUGH

FREEDOM

I am not strong till Thou hast clasped my hand,
I am not fit till by Thy side I stand;
I am not brave till Thou hast come to me;
Till Thou hast bound me fast, I am not free.
      —AUTHOR UNKNOWN

Arbor Day

THE CROSS AND THE TREE

A tree is such a sacred thing;
  I never knew just why
Until I saw my Savior, Christ,
  Stretched on a cross to die;
And heard him lift his pleading voice
  In one great, tender cry!

And now I know why poets sing
  About a common tree
As if it were a sacred thing
  Of God-like destiny.
As if each stalwart oak had roots
  That reached to Calvary!

               —WILLIAM L. STIDGER

THE HEART OF THE TREE

What does he plant who plants a tree?
He plants the friend of sun and sky;
He plants the flag of breezes free;
The shaft of beauty, towering high;
He plants a home to heaven anigh
For song and mother-croon of bird
In hushed and happy twilight heard—
The treble of heaven's harmony—
These things he plants who plants a tree.

68

What does he plant who plants a tree?
He plants cool shade and tender rain,
And seed and bud of days to be,
And years that fade and flush again:
He plants the glory of the plain;
He plants the forest's heritage;
The harvest of the coming age;
The joy that unborn eyes shall see—
These things he plants who plants a tree.

What does he plant who plants a tree?
He plants, in sap and leaf and wood,
In love of home and loyalty
And far-cast thought of civic good—
His blessing on the neighborhood
Who in the hollow of His hand
Holds all the growth of all our land—
A nation's growth from sea to sea
Stirs in his heart who plants a tree.

—H. C. BUNNER

FIR FOREST

Up above, a passing breeze
Undulates the tops of trees,
But in the green depths where I sit
Is no stir or feel of it.
No grass blade bends; no leaf turns;
No breath disturbs the peace of ferns.
Only in the cool, sweet hush
Is the call of thrush to thrush,
And all around me everywhere
A gentle sound like murmured prayer.

—ETHEL ROMIG FULLER

69

THE TEMPLE OF THE TREES

Between the erect and solemn trees
I will go down upon my knees;
    I shall not find this day
    So meet a place to pray.

Haply the beauty of this place
May work in me an answering grace,
    The stillness of the air
    Be echoed in my prayer.

The worshiping trees arise and run,
With never a swerve, toward the sun;
    So may my soul's desire
    Turn to its central fire.

With single aim they seek the light,
And scarce a twig in all their height
    Breaks out until the head
    In glory is outspread.

How strong each pillared trunk; the bark
That covers them, how smooth; and hark,
    The sweet and gentle voice
    With which the leaves rejoice!

May a like strength and sweetness fill
Desire, and thought, and steadfast will,
    When I remember these
    Fair sacramental trees!

—J. D. C. PELLOW

A FOREST MEDITATION

The green spires of the forest
    Are calling me to prayer.
The dim aisles of the forest—
    I fain would worship there.
I need not statelier altar
    Than boulders gray and old.
The swinging pine-tree censers
    Surpass the rarest gold.

Here all the nation's discord,
    The cry of battling souls,
Are merged in solemn paean,
    Whose grandeur upward rolls.
The calm of countless ages
    Subdues the strife of men;
The peace that "passeth knowledge"
    Reigns in the earth again.
                 —BERNICE HALL LEGG

ON ENTERING A FOREST

Approach this court with deference
    Lest silence strike you dumb.
The stark, judicial solitude
    Appraises all who come.

Submit your spirit; do not think
    To find recourse from these
Irrevocable judgments
    Of the parliament of trees.
                 —ELINOR LENNEN

TREE-BUILDING

A tree is built of many things—
Of soil stuff, slanting rain and hail;
Of silent snow, and skies of blue
Or lowering, of frost and gale.

Into its sinewed might are forged
No less the robin's song, the grays
Of morning mist, the sunset gold,
And rhythms of the marching days.

And by the Master built into
Cottage or templed shrine, it sings,
For him who hears, in soundless strains
The music of intangible things.

—FRANKLIN CABLE

CITY TREES

The trees along our city streets
Are lovely, gallant things;
Their roots lie deep in blackened soil,
And yet they spread their wings

Of branching green or fretted twigs
Beneath a sullen sky,
And when the wind howls banshee-like
They bow to passers-by.

In fall their leaves are bannerets
Of dusty red and gold
And fires dim that warm our hearts
Against the coming cold.

Then delicate through winter's snow
   Each silhouette still makes
Black filigree, with frostings rare
   Of silver powdered flakes.

But leafed or bare, they bravely rise
   With healing in their wings—
The trees along our city streets
   Are lovely, gallant things.
                —VERE DARGAN

WHAT DO WE PLANT?

What do we plant when we plant the tree?
We plant the ship that will cross the sea,
We plant the mast to carry the sails,
We plant the planks to withstand the gales—
The keel, the keelson, and beam and knee—
We plant the ship when we plant the tree.

What do we plant when we plant the tree?
We plant the houses for you and me.
We plant the rafters, the shingles, the floors,
We plant the studding, the lath, the doors,
The beams and siding, all parts that be;
We plant the house when we plant the tree.

What do we plant when we plant the tree?
A thousand things that we daily see.
We plant the spire that out-towers the crag,
We plant the staff for our country's flag,
We plant the shade from the hot sun free;
We plant all these when we plant the tree.
                —HENRY ABBEY

73

TREES

Oldest of friends, the trees!
Ere fire came, or iron,
Or the shimmering corn;
When the earth mist was dank,
Ere the promise of the dawn,
From the slime, from the muck—
        The trees!

Nearest of friends, the trees!
They shield us from storm
And brighten our hearths;
They bring to our tables
The autumn's fine gold;
They carol our joys
And sing to our griefs.
They cradle our young
And coffin our dead—
        The trees!

Truest of friends, the trees!
Men wander far
At a word or a nod;
Life is a grief,
Love is a chance,
Faith stumbles oft,
Joy is soon past.
Oldest of friends,
Nearest of friends,
Truest of friends,
        The trees!

—THOMAS CURTIS CLARK

74

TREE FEELINGS

I wonder if they like it—being trees?
I suppose they do. . . .
It must feel good to have the ground so flat,
And feel yourself stand right up straight like that—
So stiff in the middle—and then branch at ease,
Big boughs that arch, small ones that bend and blow,
And all those fringy leaves that flutter so.

—CHARLOTTE PERKINS STETSON

A PRAYER

Teach me, Father, how to go
Softly as the grasses grow;
Hush my soul to meet the shock
Of the wild world as a rock;
But my spirit, propt with power,
Make as simple as a flower.
Let the dry heart fill its cup,
Like a poppy looking up.

Teach me, Father, how to be
Kind and patient as a tree.
Joyfully the crickets croon
Under shady oak at noon;
Beetle, on his mission bent,
Tarries in that cooling tent.
Let me, also, cheer a nook,
Place for friendly bread and book—
Place where passing souls can rest
On the way, and be their best.

—EDWIN MARKHAM

75

PLANT A TREE

He who plants a tree
    Plants a hope.
    Rootlets up through fibres blindly grope;
Leaves unfold into horizons free.
    So man's life must climb
    From the clods of time
    Unto heavens sublime.
Canst thou prophesy, thou little tree,
What the glory of thy boughs shall be?

He who plants a tree
    Plants a joy;
    Plants a comfort that will never cloy;
Every day a fresh reality,
    Beautiful and strong,
    To whose shelter throng
    Creatures blithe with song.
If thou couldst but know, thou happy tree,
Of the bliss that shall inhabit thee!

He who plants a tree—
    He plants peace.
    Under its green curtains jargons cease.
Leaf and zephyr murmur soothingly;
    Shadows soft with sleep
    Down tired eyelids creep,
    Balm of slumber deep.
Never hast thou dreamed, thou blessed tree,
Of the benediction thou shalt be.

He who plants a tree—
    He plants love.
    Tents of coolness spreading out above
Wayfarers he may not live to see.
    Gifts that grow are best;
    Hands that bless are blest;
    Plant! life does the rest!
Heaven and earth help him who plants a tree,
And his work its own reward shall be.

                  —LUCY LARCOM

A WHITE TREE IN BLOOM

Under the yellow sun,
O can there be
Anything lovelier
Than a white tree?
Apricot, damson, quince,
Apple or plum—
Under the sun's gold fire
These smite you dumb.

Under the yellow moon,
Ghostly and fair,
Dogwood, wild-cherry tree,
Hawthorn or pear—
See how they strangely burn
Whiter than all things white;
Such trees can bring us dreams
Dreamed on no other night.

77

Under the sun, the moon,
O can there be
Anything lovelier
Than a white tree?

—John Richard Moreland

THEY ALL BELONG TO ME

Ye cannot shut the trees in,
  Ye cannot hide the hills,
Ye cannot wall the seas in,
  Ye cannot choke the rills.
The corn will only nestle
  In the broad arms of the sky,
The clover crop must wrestle
  With the common wind, or die.
And while these stores of treasure
  Are spread where I can see,
By God's high, bounteous pleasure,
  They all belong to me.

—Eliza Cook

Mother's Day

THE MOTHERS OF MEN

The bravest battle that ever was fought;
  Shall I tell you where and when?
On the maps of the world you will find it **not**;
  It was fought by the mothers of men.

Nay, not with cannon or battle shot,
  With sword or braver pen;
Nay, not with eloquent word or thought,
  From the mouths of wonderful men.

But deep in a woman's walled-up heart—
  Of woman that would not yield,
But patiently, silently bore her part—
  Lo! there in that battlefield.

No marshaling troop, no bivouac song;
  No banners to gleam and wave;
And oh! these battles they last so long—
  From babyhood to the grave!

Yet, faithful still as a bridge of stars,
  She fights in her walled-up town—
Fights on and on in the endless wars,
  Then silent, unseen—goes down.

—Joaquin Miller

79

MOTHERHOOD

Duty is a path of pain and peril,
    Roses grow on bushes thick with thorns;
A mother wears a crown of ancient travail;
    Calvary's cross a suffering Christ adorns.
                        —WILLIAM L. STIDGER

THE MOTHER OF THE HOUSE

Strength and dignity are her clothing;
    And she laugheth at the time to come.
She openeth her mouth to wisdom;
    And the law of kindness is on her tongue.
She looketh well to the ways of her household
    And eateth not the bread of idleness;
Her children rise up and call her blessed,
    Her husband also, and he praiseth her, saying:
"Many daughters have done worthily,
    But thou excelleth them all."

                        —PROVERBS 31:25-29
                        (American Standard Version)

THE GIFT

God thought to give the sweetest thing
    In his almighty power
To earth; and deeply pondering
    What it should be—one hour
In fondest joy and love of heart
    Outweighing every other,
He moved the gates of heaven apart
    And gave to earth—a Mother!
                        —AUTHOR UNKNOWN

DEAR OLD MOTHERS

I love old mothers—mothers with white hair
  And kindly eyes, and lips grown soft and sweet
With murmured blessings over sleeping babes.
  There is something in their quiet grace
That speaks the calm of Sabbath afternoons;
  A knowledge in their deep, unfaltering eyes
That far outreaches all philosophy.

Time, with caressing touch about them weaves
  The silver-threaded fairy-shawl of age,
While all the echoes of forgotten songs
  Seemed joined to lend sweetness to their speech.

Old mothers! as they pass with slow-timed step,
  Their trembling hands cling gently to youth's strength.
Sweet mothers!—as they pass, one sees again
  Old garden-walks, old roses, and old loves.

—CHARLES S. ROSS

MOTHERHOOD

They walk with surer step the paths of men
And choose with finer grace the common way;
They learn their patience from the harder day
And, oft defeated, rise in strength again.

Their eyes guard all the wisdom of the years,
Their lips still cling to each forgotten song;
Forgetting yesterday's unmeasured wrong,
They hope anon against tomorrow's fears.

81

Their hands still soothe the tortured, fevered brow,
Their hearts still pour the blood that builds the race,
And still before their radiant, wistful face
Earth's generations in deep reverence bow.

And men shall keep their faith that God is good
While Love still spends itself in Motherhood.
                              —KARL M. CHWOROWSKY

THE NAME OF MOTHER

The noblest thoughts my soul can claim,
The holiest words my tongue can frame,
Unworthy are to frame the name
    More sacred than all other.
An infant when her love first came,
A man, I find it just the same:
Reverently I breathe her name—
    The blessed name of Mother.
                         —GEORGE GRIFFITH FETTER

MOTHER'S LOVE

A mother's love—how sweet the name!
    What is a mother's love?
A noble, pure, and tender flame,
    Enkindled from above.
To bless a heart of earthly mold;
The warmest love that can grow old—
    This is mother's love.
                              —F. MONTGOMERY

MOTHER

For others she may not be fair—
Her furrowed cheeks, her faded hair;
To me she is a treasure rare,
    My Mother.
Her charm how can I but confess!
For there's no other face can bless
And keep my heart from loneliness,
As that dear face
    Of Mother.

So long ago for Mother, young,
The wedding bells were gaily rung;
So long ago glad songs were sung
    For Mother;
And still, to me, she's worthy quite
Of all that's lovely, sweet, and bright.
She's queen today, by her own right,
Queen of my heart,
    My Mother.

               —THOMAS CURTIS CLARK

THE PIONEER MOTHER

Upon a jolting wagonseat she rode
Across the trackless prairie to the west,
Or trudged beside the oxen with a goad,
A sleeping child clasped tightly to her breast.
Frail flesh rebelling, but spirit never—
What tales the dark could tell of women's tears!—
Her bravery incentive to endeavor;
Her laughter spurring strong men past their fears.

83

O to her valor and comeliness
A commonwealth today owes its white domes
Of state, its fields, its highways and its homes;
Its cities wrested from the wilderness,
And bends in memory above the hand
That gentled, woman-wise, a savage land.
—ETHEL ROMIG FULLER

QUEEN OF THE WORLD

The Mother in her office holds the key
Of the soul; and she it is who stamps the coin
Of character, and makes the being, who would be a
    savage
But for her gentle cares, a Christian man
Then crown her Queen of the World!
—FROM AN OLD PLAY

From MY TRUST

A picture memory brings to me:
I look across the years and see
Myself beside my mother's knee.

I feel her gentle hand restrain
My selfish moods, and know again
A child's blind sense of wrong and pain.

But wiser now, a man gray grown,
My childhood's needs are better known,
My mother's chastening love I own.
—JOHN GREENLEAF WHITTIER

84

MY MOTHER

If I should paint thy portrait, mother dear,
I could not picture your kind look and ways,
Your constancy and care, through childhood days;
In lonely hours how oft I've wished you near!
I've missed your counsel wise, and smile of cheer.
These words are futile, though I speak your praise,
No tribute ever sung or said, portrays
Your steadfast love and faith from year to year.

All undeserving of a love like yours,
A love that never failed me, that endures;
Today I'll wear this crimson flower for you,
My childhood's trustful faith again renew.
With contrite heart, I humbly kneel, and pray,
"God bless and keep you," mother dear, today.
—BERTHA NOLAN

WONDROUS MOTHERHOOD

Thank God! for that lovely spirit
That makes motherhood akin.
They have known the way of travail.
They have known the pangs of pain.
They have compassed hope and sorrow.
They have had both tears and joy.
That is why a glowing radiance
Shines in all they say and do.
That is why they are the blessed,
Why we hail them far and wide
Dearest of all God's creations,
Great and wondrous motherhood.
—AUTHOR UNKNOWN

85

MOTHER—A PORTRAIT

Her hands have much
Of Christlike touch.

Her smile on one
Is benison.

Her silver hair,
A halo rare.

Her step, a sound
On holy ground.

Her dear face lined,
But kind—kind.

Of women, best
And loveliest.

—Ethel Romig Fuller

MOTHER

There is not a grand inspiring thought,
There is not a truth by wisdom taught,
There is not a feeling pure and high,
That may not be read in a mother's eye.

There are teachings in earth, and sky, and air,
The heavens the glory of God declare;
But louder than voice, beneath, above,
He is heard to speak through a mother's love.

—Emily Taylor

O MOTHERS OF THE HUMAN RACE

O Mothers of the Human Race,
　Who, in the birthing of our breath,
The uttermost of suffering face,
　And touch the very hem of death,
Will you not mother all mankind
Into one all-maternal mind?

O Mothers of the Human Race,
　Whose milk is universal bread,
As all-sustaining as the grace
　Of the heart's universal red,
Will you not feed us with the food
Of love for all the human brood?

O Mothers of the Human Race,
　Protectors of our infant years,
Who wooed us to our first embrace,
　And taught us laughter out of tears,
Teach us the gesture and the glee
Of the world-love that is to be.

　　　　　　　　　—ROBERT WHITAKER

LOVE'S TRIBUTE

I wear a snow-white rose today
　In sacred memory,
In silent tribute to the love
　My mother bore for me.

The fairest flower will fade and die,
　But deeds live on for aye;
A life well lived shows proof of love
　Far more than words we say.

87

So I would live from day to day
That all my life shall be
A living tribute to that love—
A faithful memory.

—LORENA W. STURGEON

From THE PRINCESS

I loved her, one
Not learned, save in gracious household ways,
Nor perfect, nay, but full of tender wants,
No Angel, but a dearer being, all dipt
In Angel instincts, breathing Paradise,
Interpreter between the Gods and men,
Who look'd all native to her place, and yet
On tiptoe seem'd to touch upon a sphere
Too gross to tread, and all male minds perforce
Sway'd to her from their orbits as they moved,
And girdled her with music. Happy he
With such a mother! faith in womenkind
Beats with his blood, and trust in all things high
Comes easy to him, and tho' he trip and fall,
He shall not blind his soul with clay.

—ALFRED TENNYSON

A MOTHER'S NAME

No painter's brush, nor poet's pen
    In justice to her fame
Has ever reached half high enough
    To write a mother's name.

—AUTHOR UNKNOWN

MOTHER LOVE

I bent my ears to a lily's cup,
  And thought that it spoke to me
By the stainless white of its petals light,
  Of a mother's purity.

To the heart of a red, red rose I crushed
  And it seemed that within my eyes
There was shadowed the gleam of the crimson stream
  Of a mother's sacrifice.

I considered the sun and the moon and the stars,
  The winds, and the tides of the sea,
And found in the span of their beautiful plan
  All a mother's constancy.

Then I lifted my eyes to a hilltop lone,
  Where Love hung high on a tree.
And lo, it was there I could best compare
  My mother's love for me!

—JANIE ALFORD

MOTHER

Each day to her a miracle,
  Fresh from her Father's hand;
She bore with patience every grief
  She could not understand.

The ears of others were her own,
  Their joys of hers a part;
The lonely never were alone
  Close to her tender heart.

89

No more along life's rugged path
Her tired feet must roam,
For she, who made of home a Heaven,
Wakes—to find Heaven her home!

—AUTHOR UNKNOWN

MOTHERS

I think God took the fragrance of a flower,
A pure white flower, which blooms not for world praise,
But which makes sweet and beautiful some bower;
The compassion of the dew, which gently lays
Reviving freshness on the fainting earth,
And gives to all the tired things new birth;
The steadfastness and radiance of stars,
Which lift the soul above confining bars;
The gladness of fair dawns; the sunset's peace;
Contentment which from "trivial rounds" asks no release;
The life which finds its greatest joy in deeds of love for
    others—
I think God took these precious things, and made of them—
    the Mothers.

—AUTHOR UNKNOWN

Memorial Day

HOW SHALL WE HONOR THEM?

How shall we honor them, our Deathless Dead?
With strew of laurel and the stately tread?
With blaze of banners brightening overhead?
Nay, not alone these cheaper praises bring:
They will not have this easy honoring.

How shall we honor them, our Deathless Dead?
How keep their mighty memories alive?
In him who feels their passion, they survive!
Flatter their souls with deeds, and all is said!
—Edwin Markham

AFTERMATH

Not this spring shall return again,
Not this my city rise,
Not my son from his flag-draped bier
Stand up with laughing eyes.

Another year, another city, another boy shall be.
New men will sing new songs.
New right shall men establish. . . . But
Irreparable are:
This ravished spring,
This city razed,
This my son dead.
—Margaret McCulloch

BITTER QUESTION

How sound are ye sleeping, comrades,
  So deeply that air raids pass
Like shadows on silver mirrors,
  Like breathing on polished glass?

How deep are ye dreaming, comrades,
  So raptly that raiders go
From France to the spires of London
  And none of you ever know?

Ah, lads, I have named you over,
  Remembering how ye died,
So wearily full of slumber—
  Mute pawns of a nation's pride!

How sound are ye sleeping, comrades,
  Too deeply to ever ken
The bells of the world are ringing
  For anguish and war again?
                    —ARTHUR R. MACDOUGALL, JR.

THERE WILL BE PEACE

The light will shine again; it cannot die,
For truth can never pass as winters go
With lengthening twilight, and uncertain snow
That faintly flutters through a leaden sky.
There will be peace at last, and you and I
Will find before the early tulips blow,
A field to plant against the summer's glow
And yellow harvest when the wild geese fly.
                    —MARGARET MILLER PETTENGILL

MEMORIAL DAY

I heard a cry in the night from a far-flung host,
From a host that sleeps through the years the last long sleep,
By the Meuse, by the Marne, in the Argonne's shattered wood,
In a thousand rose-thronged churchyards through our land.
Sleeps! Do they sleep! I know I heard their cry,
Shrilling along the night like a trumpet blast:

"We died," they cried, "for a dream. Have ye forgot?
We dreamed of a world reborn whence wars had fled,
Where swords were broken in pieces and guns were rust,
Where the poor man dwelt in quiet, the rich in peace,
And children played in the streets, joyous and free.
We thought we could sleep content in a task well done;
But the rumble of guns rolls over us, iron upon iron
Sounds from the forge where are fashioned guns anew;

"New fleets spring up in new seas, and under the wave
Stealthy new terrors swarm, with emboweled death.
Fresh cries of hate ring out loud from the demagogue's throat,
While greed reaches out afresh to grasp new lands.
Have we died in vain? Is our dream denied?
You men who live on the earth we bought with our woe,
Will ye stand idly by while they shape new wars,
Or will ye rise, who are strong, to fulfill our dream,
To silence the demagogue's voice, to crush the fools
Who play with blood-stained toys that crowd new graves?
We call, we call in the night, will ye hear and heed?"

In the name of our dead will we hear? Will we grant them
   sleep?

—WILLIAM E. BROOKS

93

THUS SPEAK THE SLAIN

No longer heed we war and strife,
No longer pace your petty life;
We are the dead, O ye who live,
We are the dead who life did give
    That peace might reign!

Bring us your wreath and wordy praise;
We note them, yes—but we whose days
Are gone cry from the graves we fill,
"Where is the peace, the love, good will
    We died to gain?"

Shall we forever cry from sod,
"What have we perished for, O God?
Died we that men might scheme and plot
And riches heap while virtues rot—
    Died we in vain?"

If ye who live heed not our cry
And rise not from your muck and sty,
Our souls shall march, a phalanx stern,
God's searing truth on you to burn!
    Thus speak the slain.

—CARL HOLLIDAY

SILENT TESTIMONY

Under the crosses white on a foreign meadow
Mute they are lying who marched in the spring-sweet sun.
Nothing is here of the life, the joy, the loving,
Before a war was won.

—CATHERINE PARMENTER

WE WHO ARE DEAD

We who are dead, we cannot sleep
  Beneath the crosses, row on row.
We hear the common folk who weep;
  We feel the dirk-thrusts of their woe.

We who are dead, who fought for you,
  We cannot rest in Flanders field.
We died to make a world anew,
  And now you take the sword and shield.

We who are dead, comrade and friend,
  We call to you to do the task
We died to do—to make an end
  Of war and want; just this we ask,
We who are dead.
                                    —PAUL L. BENJAMIN

WE WHOM THE DEAD HAVE NOT FORGIVEN

I cry to the mountains; I cry to the sea—
I cry to the forest to cover me
From the terror of the invisible throng

With marching feet the whole day long—
The whole night long,
Beating the accent of their wrong.

We whom the Dead have not forgiven
Must hear forever that ominous beat,
For the free, light, rippled air of heaven
Is burdened now with dead men's feet:

Feet that make solid the fluid space,
Feet that make weary the tireless wind,
Feet that leave grime on the moon's white face—
Black is the moon for us who have sinned!

And the mountains will not cover us,
Nor yet the forest nor the sea;
No storm of human restlessness
Can wake the tide or bend the tree.

Forever and ever until we die,
Through the once sweet air and the once blue sky
The thud of feet—the invisible throng,
Beating the accent of their wrong.

—SARA BARD FIELD

HIGH FLIGHT

Oh! I have slipped the surly bonds of Earth,
And danced the skies on laughter-silvered wings;
Sunward I've climbed, and joined the tumbling mirth
Of sun-split clouds—and done a hundred things
You have not dreamed of—wheeled and soared and swung
High in the sunlit silence. Hov'ring there,
I've chased the shouting wind along, and flung
My eager craft through footless halls of air. . . .
Up, up the long delirious, burning blue
I've topped the wind-swept heights with easy grace,
Where never lark or even eagle flew—
And while with silent, lifting mind I've trod
The high untrespassed sanctity of space,
Put out my hand and touched the face of God.

—JOHN MAGEE

TOWARD A TRUE PEACE

The old world staggers, but a young, triumphant
   world is born.
Before the Tower of Babel, sound a clear, resurgent horn
And prophesy the jubilant dawn when a true peace
   will come!
Make the will of the world your trumpet, the heart
   of the world your drum!
             —LUCIA TRENT AND RALPH CHEYNEY

COMRADE, REMEMBER

Comrade, within your tent of clay
   Waiting the march of ghostly legions,
The dead can speak. What do they say
   As they march to the heavenly regions?

Comrade, your peace is still and deep
   As God's own flesh burned to gray embers.
How can I honor you who sleep
   Where only God himself remembers?

"Comrade," he says, "I am not dead,
   Nor is my last strange sentence spoken
As long as comrades mark the tread
   Of crippled feet and bodies broken.

"Remember them, and I shall die.
   Remember them and then, forgetting
Us dead, show them the clean white sky
   With the sun of peace never setting."
             —RAYMOND KRESENSKY

97

IN FLANDERS FIELDS

In Flanders fields the poppies blow
Between the crosses, row on row,
    That mark our place; and in the sky,
    The larks, still bravely singing, fly
Scarce heard amid the guns below.

We are the dead. Short days ago
We lived, felt dawn, saw sunset glow,
    Loved and were loved, and now we lie
    In Flanders fields.

Take up our quarrel with the foe:
To you from failing hands we throw
    The torch; be yours to hold it high.
    If ye break faith with us who die
We shall not sleep, though poppies grow
    In Flanders fields.

—JOHN McCRAE

SCAPEGOATS

The young men die in battle,
    The old men sleep in bed.
The tortured earth of Europe
    Is furrowed deep with red.

The old men sat conferring
    With smile and scheme and lie—
And so the old men blundered,
    And so the young men die.

—ELEANOR D. BREED

98

ON A WORLD WAR BATTLEFIELD

They are not dead, the soldiers fallen here;
   Their spirits walk throughout the world today;
They still proclaim their message far and near:
   Might is not right, God's truth must have its way!

The cold, damp soil cannot these heroes hide;
   Those knightly lads who did not fear to die
That liberty and freedom still might bide;
   Weep not for them, though here they lowly lie.

Go forth and tell their message to the world;
   In vain their fight, in vain the foe withstood,
Unless above all kingdoms be unfurled
   The pure white flag of love and brotherhood.
                —THOMAS CURTIS CLARK

IF THESE ENDURE

If these endure when all the old world crashes,
   If these stars shine above the last gun's roll:
Strength to raise brave new towers on sacred ashes,
   Courage to build new mansions for the soul;
Faith to point loftier spires to kindlier heavens,
   Wisdom to soar above the fear of fear;
Beauty to feed the earth with nobler leavens,
   And rear the Holy City now and here;
Peace that shall yield no more to greed's dictation,
   Freedom from want and loneliness and pain,
Love like a white flag over every nation—
   If these endure we have not fought in vain.
                —LILITH LORRAINE

99

FOR THOSE WHO DIED

How crowded is the heavenly House of Light
With those who from the cruel wars have come—
Bright, glowing youths of fresh and vital breath
Who thought so lightly of their lives—and death!
No more shall they awake to martial drum,
No more march fearless through the warlike night.
We sent them forth, they did not ask us why;
But on they went—in tears we saw them go.

Across the seas they sped and took their stand,
While we, in our own safe and sheltered land,
Bade them be strong to grapple with the foe;
They heard our voice, and clave the angry sky. . . .

How crowded is the heavenly House of Light
With those who marched—for us—into the night!
                    —THOMAS CURTIS CLARK

FROM BEYOND

Pity us not
Because we tried to battle and to go
Like men upon the beckoning of Death,
Because through all your life you may not know
The pain we suffered with one dying breath.
The gnawing agony, the burning woe.

Pity us not
Because, torn from the might of blasting shell,
Our bodies never find a place of rest,
No stone where those we loved may come to tell
The sorrow that is weighted in their breast.

100

But pity us
Because the earth is lovely still and fair,
And there is still the spring of which to dream,
Because the stalwart poplars proudly bare
Their beauty to the April moonlight's gleam.

And pity us
Because men desecrate this shrine of God,
Ravage the altar of earth's loveliness,
Sow seeds of bondage in the bitter sod
To reap the grain of torture and distress.

Pity us, too,
Because the world prepares another hell
For sons of ours to rage and suffer through,
For sons of ours to die by gas and shell,
For sons of ours to know the pain we knew.

Pity us
Because a truer and more godlike way
Men will not even seek to know or find,
Nor hail the coming of a kinder day—
O God, that men will be so blind!

—LUCIA TRENT

THE CRIMINALITY OF WAR

One to destroy is murder by the law,
And gibbets keep the lifted hand in awe;
To murder thousands takes a specious name,
War's glorious art, and gives immortal fame.

—EDWARD YOUNG

101

MARY AT THE CROSS

And Mary stood beside the cross! Her soul
Pierced with the self-same wound that rent His side
Who hung thereon. She watched Him, as He died.
Her son! Saw Him paying the cruel toll
Exacted by the law, and unbelief,
Since He their evil will had dared defy.
There stood the mother helpless in her grief,
Beside the cross, and saw her first-born die!

How many mothers in how many lands
Have bowed with Mary in her agony,
In silence borne the wrath of war's commands,
When every hill is made a Calvary!

O pity, Lord, these mothers of the slain,
And grant their dead shall not have died in vain.
—CLYDE McGEE

WHY

The men of the earth said: "We must war
  As the men of the earth have warred·
'Tis ours to wield on the battlefield
  The unrelenting sword."
But they who had seen the valiant die,
The fathers of men, they answered, "Why?"

The men of the earth said: "We must arm,
  For so we would reveal
The nobler part of the human heart,
  The love of the nation's weal."
But they who had sung their lullaby,
The mothers of men, they answered, "Why?"

102

The men of the earth said: "We must fight,
   For so the fit survive;
By the jungle law of fang and claw
   The strong are kept alive."
But a crippled, cankered progeny,
The sons of the culls, they answered, "Why?"

The men of the earth said: "We must fall,
   And falling build the road
O'er which the race with quickening pace
   Can find its way to God."
But down from a cross uplifted high,
The Savior of men, he answered, "Why?"
        —ROBERT FREEMAN

A MOTHER BEFORE A SOLDIER'S MONUMENT

Was it for this I braved a pathless, dark
And chilling void, in travail while the hiss
Of Death grew loud and near; from that abyss
To stumble back, enfolding in the arc
Of love-warm arms an infant life—a spark
I fanned to ruddy glow? Was it for this
I succored childish needs—healed with a kiss
Each wound that left, on flesh or pride, its mark?

Ah yes, for this I led my stalwart son
In paths of rectitude; abhorring vice
And choosing honor's way, he tossed the draft
That brimmed Youth's cup. . . . Bereft and old, I run
Through War's red ledger—scan the costly price
I paid for laurel wreath and marble shaft!
        —WINNIE LYNCH ROCKETT

103

THE STARRED MOTHER

Is there a madness underneath the sun
More strange, more terrible? or any one
More pitiful than this, that for a star
A mother sells her flesh and blood to war?

A son for slaughter, and a star for praise!
Nor this the total madness of our days,
A son to slay some other mother's son,
And by such murder mother's blessing won!

The Hindu mother, by the Ganges tide
Drowning her babe, heartbroken, but with pride,
Poor blind purveyor to a Saurian feast,
Still spares her babe from murder's maw, at least.

Is there debauchery more deep than this?
The State betraying mothers with a kiss?
Bribing the Marys of the world to sell,
For tinseled star, their flesh and blood to hell!

—ROBERT WHITAKER

THE REAPERS

Red are the hands of the Reapers,
  And the harvest is so white!
Red are the feet that are treading
  The threshing floors by night:
And, on the young brows, dripping
  As with the dews of morn,
Deep rose-red are the woundings,
  Like scars of a crown of thorn.

Tired, so many, with reaping,
   Tired with treading the grain,
Still they lie, in their sleeping,
   Low in the Valley of Pain—
Never again to be quaffing
   The joy of life, like wine;
Never again to be laughing
   In youth's glad hour divine.

Birds shall sing in the branches,
   Children dance by the shore;
But they who shared the red reaping
   Shall come back nevermore.
Let whoso can forget them,
   Walking life's noisy ways;
We who have looked on the Reapers
   Go quietly, all our days.
               —LAUCHLAN MACLEAN WATT

THE LAMENT OF THE VOICELESS

"Wars are to be," they say, they blindly say,
Nor strive to end them. Had we eyes to see
The ghosts that walk across the fields of slain,
We might behold by each boy soldier's corpse
An endless line who mourn his fateful doom.

"Who are you?" asking, we might hear these words:
"We are the men and women not to be,
Because the father of our line was slain,
Cut off untimely. Brave he was and strong;
His heritage were ours had he not been
The food of slaughter in a wanton war."

105

Boy soldier, sleep, by fireside mourned;
By neighbor comrades, half ashamed of life,
When death claims him who went that they might stay.
Boy soldier, sleep; if ever these forget,
You still are mourned by that long line unborn
Who might have been but for the waste of war.
They mourn for you, your sons who never were.
                                        —LAURA BELL EVERETT

UNKNOWN SOLDIER

Flowers for you, O Glory's son, war's prey!
How long, how long since you were laid
To guarded rest where a nation's shrine is made!
Nor care nor fighting touch you there.

A pretty spot, Soldier, above your head,
But you, brave lad, are dead . . . are dead.
And in this world you gallantly forswore
Already leer and snarl the wolves of war,
While folly, hatred, lust and greed
Contend much as before.

Courage and the high heart were yours.
Then shall we patriots supinely heap
Your tomb with wreaths of fame
(Your price for peace now half forgot), and weep
Old tears that Hero is your only name
We know? Nay, lad! We valiant rise to keep
The faith with you and all youth, lest war number
All lovely things of life and dear
With sons he's sent to fatal slumber!
                                        —ALTA BOOTH DUNN

IT IS NOT TOO LATE

Mothers and fathers of sons, what will you be saying
When the crimson sickle slashes the living grain
And the boy with the morning smile for whom you
are praying
Lies stark in the terrible rain?

What will you say when his voice is crying, crying,
Through the soundless night, throughout the
unechoing day:
"Why did you let us go to our dying, dying,
In the May of our lives, in the May?"

Mothers and fathers of sons, do you hear that rattle?
It is not too late to rescue ten million sons.
Join in humanity's salvation battle
For a world without greed, without guns.

—LUCIA TRENT

YOUTH

We have heard the trumpets calling Youth,
We have seen their proud reply,
Laughing as they leapt to die,
Boyhood in their battle cry;
We have heard the world's tears falling
For slain youth.

Still a sterner strife is calling Youth,
Madness beats upon the gates
Of old selfishness; age prates,
Cavils, queries, hesitates;
Nearer roars the storm, appalling
All but Youth—

107

Youth that hears diviner voices, Youth
That has faith in brotherhood,
Courage to attempt a good
Only visioned yet, that would
Build a world where life rejoices,
      Generous Youth.

          —KATHARINE LEE BATES

IN THE NAME OF OUR SONS

Above the graves of countless millions slain
The people cry: "By their grim sacrifice—
Whose lives, free-given, we cannot despise—
We vow, in tears: It shall not be again!"

          —DOROTHY GOULD

MEMORIAL

Still sleeps the unknown soldier
   His long and dreamless sleep,
While loud with prayer we reaffirm
   The faith he died to keep—

In graveyards without number,
   Upon the nameless stone,
The heart stops to remember,
   Then goes ahead, alone. . . .

Today we pause in tribute;
   Tomorrow we will pass—
The grave marked only by the green
   Memorial of grass!

          —MAE WINKLER GOODMAN

WE WHO ARE ABOUT TO DIE

We who are about to die salute each other in the old way. Again we marshal conscripts, multiply planes and ships, drug ourselves with hate, and whip our allies into line. Nothing has changed.

We who "won victory" in war know that we have already lost another peace. Once more we have decided to decide to fight, chosen to trust in defense that compounds jeopardy. Nothing has changed.

We who "saved freedom" forge in the hot fires of fear the chains of new slavery. Bound hand and foot, we chant the old song of death while our foes answer in antiphonal chorus. Nothing has changed.

We who are about to die salute each other in the old way. Nothing has changed, but God has grown weary of the cycle. Lifting the lid on the atom, He says: "Choose life or death, but choose!"
—HAROLD E. FEY

LAST THOUGHTS OF A FIGHTING MAN [1]

Look, God, I have never spoken to You,
But now I want to say, "How do You do?"
You see, God, they told me You didn't exist,
And like a fool I believed all this.

[1] These lines were written by an unknown American soldier in the Second World War serving overseas and found by the stretcher-bearers who carried his lifeless body off the field of action. Apparently they had just been written.

109

Last night from a shell hole I saw Your sky—
I figured right then they had told me a lie.
Had I taken time to see the thing You made,
I'd known they weren't calling a spade a spade.

I wonder, God, if You'd shake my hand,
Somehow I feel You would understand.
Funny I had to come to this hellish place
Before I had time to see your face.

Well, I guess there isn't much more to say,
But I'm sure glad, God, I met You today.
I guess the zero hour will soon be here,
But I'm not afraid since I know You're near.

The signal! Well, God, I'll have to go.
I like You lots and I want You to know.
Look now, this will be a horrible fight;
Who knows, I may come to Your House tonight.

Though I wasn't friendly with You before,
I wonder, God, if You'd wait at Your door.
Look, I'm crying! Me! Shedding tears!
I wish I had known You these many years.

Well, I will have to go now, God; good-by!
Strange, since I met you, I'm not afraid to die.

—Author Unknown

IN MEMORIAM

No tranquil ordered day of ours
    But some lad paid its bloody price;
No joy that brims our hands but lives
    By reason of dire sacrifice;

110

No love but that fulfills itself
    Upon their broken loves; no nights
Of quiet sleep but others wept
    Their cost on Golgotha's grim heights.

They gave their safety for our own;
    For us they fought and bled and died;
Drained sorrow's cup, took on themselves
    The anguish of the Crucified;
Bought our slow ease with piercèd hands,
    Our laughter with their piteous cries;
Our singing with pale silenced lips,
    Our wonder with their blinded eyes.

Their names are writ on every flower,
    On every tree their sign is set.
Birds are their words; by day and night
    The very stones cry out our debt.
We will keep faith! Our hands take up
    The charge their dying hands let fall—
And in an everlasting peace
    We build their proud memorial.

—ADA JACKSON

Flag Day

THE AMERICAN FLAG

When Freedom from her mountain height
  Unfurled her standard to the air,
She tore the azure robe of night,
  And set the stars of glory there;

She mingled with its gorgeous dyes
The milky baldric of the skies,
And striped its pure, celestial white
With streakings of the morning light.

Then, from his mansion in the sun
She called her eagle bearer down,
And gave into his mighty hand,
The symbol of her chosen land.

.   .   .   .

Flag of the free heart's hope and home!
  By angel hands to valor given;
Thy stars have lit the welkin dome,
  And all thy hues were born in heaven.
Forever float that standard sheet!
  Where breathes the foe but falls before us,
With Freedom's soil beneath our feet,
  And Freedom's banner streaming o'er us?

—JOSEPH RODMAN DRAKE

OUR FLAG

Only a bit of color
  Waving upon the street;
Only a wind-whipped pennant
  Where the band plays shrill and sweet.

Yet the soldier's heart beats faster,
  And proud is the sailor's eye,
And the citizen's step is quickened
  When our flag is passing by.

Only a bit of color,
  Did I hear a body say?
True be the hearts that greet it
  Wherever it waves today!

Back of that bit of color
  Lies a nation's history,
And ahead of our splendid banner—
  Who knows what there yet may be?
        —FRANCES CROSBY HAMLET

From SONG OF LIBERTY

Lead on, lead on, America,
  And set thy brothers free!
Through life and death and round the world,
  O Flag, I'll follow thee!
Lead on, lead on! our hearts are great
  With purpose born of God,
For we are pledged to liberty
  On this, our deathless sod.

  . . . .

America, thou promised land,
  Thy dreams and hopes are mine,
And I will break thy sacred bread
  And drink thy living wine.
O God, our source of liberty,
  Stretch forth thy mighty hand
And bless the life of her we love,
  The free man's chosen land.

—Louise Ayres Garnett

I AM WHAT YOU MAKE ME

I am whatever you make me, nothing more.

I am your belief in yourself, your dream of what a people may become.

I live a changing life, a life of moods and passions, of heart-breaks and tired muscles.

Sometimes I am strong with pride, when workmen do an honest piece of work, fitting the rails together truly.

Sometimes I droop, for then purpose has gone from me, and cynically I play the coward;

But always I am all that you hope to be, and have the courage to try for.

I am song and fear, struggle and panic, and ennobling hope.

I am the day's work of the weakest man, and the largest dream of the most daring.

I am what you make me, nothing more.

I swing before your eyes as a bright gleam of color,

A symbol of yourself,

A pictured suggestion of that big thing which makes this nation.

My stars and my stripes are your dream and your labors.

They are bright with cheer, brilliant with courage, firm with faith, because you have made them so out of your hearts.

—Franklin K. Lane

114

OUR FLAG FOREVER

She's up there—Old Glory—where lightnings are sped;
She dazzles the nations with ripples of red;
And she'll wave for us living, or droop o'er us dead—
    The flag of our country forever!

She's up there—Old Glory—how bright the stars stream!
And the stripes like red signals of liberty gleam!
And we dare for her, living, or dream the last dream,
    'Neath the flag of our country forever!

She's up there—Old Glory—no tyrant-dealt scars,
No blur on her brightness, no stain on her stars!
The brave blood of heroes hath crimsoned her bars.
    She's the flag of our country forever!
        —FRANK L. STANTON

THE FLAG GOES BY

Hats off!
Along the street there comes
A blare of bugles, a ruffle of drums,
A flash of color beneath the sky
Hats off!
The flag is passing by!

Blue, and crimson, and white it shines,
Over the steel-tipped, ordered lines.
Hats off!
The colors before us fly;
But more than the flag is passing by.

115

Sea fights and land fights, grim and great,
Fought to make and to save the state;
Weary marches and sinking ships;
Cheers of victory on dying lips;

Days of plenty, and years of peace,
March of a strong land's swift increase;
Equal justice, right and law,
Stately honor and reverent awe;

Sign of a Nation, great and strong,
To ward her people from foreign wrong;
Pride, and glory, and honor, all
Live in the colors to stand or fall.

Hats off!
Along the street there comes
A blare of bugles, a ruffle of drums;
And loyal hearts are beating high.
Hats off!
The flag is passing by!

—H. H. Bennett

THE FLAG SPEAKS

Brave men have followed
My irresistible
Beauty and magic:
Comradeship, loyalty,
High hearts' devotion
Shone in their faces
Fixed on my stars.

116

Tattered and blood-stained
In halls of honor,
I dream of my lovers
Whom I misled.

Cleansed of the blood-stain,
In the new morning
I call afar.

Not in one land alone,
Not in one tongue alone,
Not through one only flag,
Comes the new Word.

Leave the old death-dealing,
Leave the old fearing,
Lead on to life-giving—
Life, more abundant life—
Now it is day.

Never again in wars
Float my stripes, flash my stars:
I am the flag of life,
Sister of every flag
In the wide world.

—EMILY GREENE BALCH

STAND BY THE FLAG

Stand by the Flag! Its stars like meteors gleaming,
  Have lighted Arctic icebergs, southern seas,
And shone responsive to the stormy beaming
  Of old Arcturus and the Pleiades.

Stand by the Flag! Its stripes have streamed in glory,
   To foes a fear, to friends a festal robe,
And spread in rhythmic lines the sacred story
   Of Freedom's triumphs over all the globe.

Stand by the Flag! On land and ocean billow
   By it your fathers stood unmoved and true,
Living defended; dying, from their pillow,
   With their last blessing passed it on to you.

Stand by the Flag! Immortal heroes bore it
   Through sulphurous smoke, deep moat and armed defense;
And their imperial Shades still hover o'er it,
   A guard celestial from Omnipotence.
                    —JOHN NICHOLS WILDER

MY COUNTRY IS THE WORLD

My country is the world;
My flag with stars impearled
   Fills all the skies.
All the round earth I claim,
Peoples of every name;
And all inspiring fame
   My heart would prize.

Mine are all lands and seas,
All flowers, shrubs and trees,
   All life's design;
My heart within me thrills
For all uplifted hills,
And for all streams and rills;
   The world is mine.

118

All men are of my kin,
Since every man has been
    Blood of my blood;
I glory in the grace
And strength of every race
And joy in every trace
    Of brotherhood.

The days of pack and clan
Shall yield to love of man,
    War flags be furled;
We shall be done with hate,
And strife of state with state,
When man with man shall mate
    O'er all the world.

—ROBERT WHITAKER

THE OLD FLAG

Off with your hat as the flag goes by!
    And let the heart have its say;
You're man enough for a tear in your eye
    That you will not wipe away.

You're man enough for a thrill that goes
    To your very finger-tips—
Ay! the lump just then in your throat that rose
    Spoke more than your parted lips.

Lift up the boy on your shoulder high,
    And show him the faded shred;
Those stripes would be red as the sunset sky
    If death could have dyed them red.

119

Off with your hat as the flag goes by!
Uncover the youngster's head;
Teach him to hold it holy and high
For the sake of its sacred dead.

—H. C. BUNNER

I AM THE FLAG

I am a composite being of all the people of America.
I am the union if you are united.
I am one and indivisible if you are undivided.
I am as strong as the weakest link.
I am an emblem of your country.
I am a symbol of a shadow of the real.
I am a sign pointing to past achievements.
I am a promise of greater things for the future.
I am what you make me.
I am purity if you are pure.
I am bravery if you are brave.
I am loyalty if you are loyal.

. . . .

I am honor if you are honorable.
I am goodness if you are good.
I am hope if you are hopeful.
I am truth if you are true.

. . . .

I am the Constitution.
I am law and order.
I am tolerance or intolerance as you force me to be.
I am liberty as you understand liberty.
I am as a pillar of fire by night, but you must
    provide the fuel.

. . . .

120

I march at the head of the column, but you must
    carry me on.

.   .   .   .

I stand for greater and more glorious achievement
    than can be found in recorded history, but
    you must be my inspiration.
I AM THE FLAG.

—LAWRENCE M. JONES

THERE IS A LAND

There is a land, of every land the pride,
Beloved by Heaven o'er all the world beside;
Where brighter suns dispense serener light,
And milder moons imparadise the night;
A land of beauty, virtue, valor, truth,
Time-tutored age, and love-exalted youth.
Where shall that land, that spot of earth be found?
Art thou a man? a patriot? look around!
Oh! thou shalt find, howe'er thy footsteps roam,
That land thy country, and that spot thy home.

—JAMES MONTGOMERY

Independence Day

THE FATHERLAND

Where is the true man's fatherland?
  Is it where he by chance is born?
  Doth not the yearning spirit scorn
In such scant borders to be spanned?
Oh, yes! his fatherland must be
As the blue heaven wide and free!

Is it alone where freedom is,
  Where God is God and man is man?
  Doth he not claim a broader span
For the soul's love of home than this?
Oh, yes! his fatherland must be
As the blue heaven wide and free!

Where'er a human heart doth wear
  Joy's myrtle-wreath or sorrow's gyves,
  Where'er a human spirit strives
After a life more true and fair,
There is the true man's birthplace grand,
His is a world-wide fatherland!

Where'er a single slave doth pine,
  Where'er one man may help another—
  Thank God for such a birthright, brother—
That spot of earth is thine and mine!
There is the true man's birthplace grand,
His is a world-wide fatherland!

—JAMES RUSSELL LOWELL

LANDING OF THE PILGRIM FATHERS
IN NEW ENGLAND

The breaking waves dashed high
　On a stern and rock-bound coast,
And the woods against a stormy sky
　Their giant branches tossed;

And the heavy night hung dark
　The hills and waters o'er,
When a band of exiles moored their bark
　On the wild New England shore.

Not as the conqueror comes,
　They, the true-hearted, came;
Not with roll of stirring drums,
　And the trumpet that sings of fame;

Not as the flying come,
　In silence and in fear;
They shook the depths of the desert gloom
　With their hymns of lofty cheer.

.　　.　　.　　.　　.　　.　　.

What sought they thus afar?
　Bright jewels of the mine?
The wealth of seas, the spoils of war?—
　They sought a faith's pure shrine!

Ay, call it holy ground,
　The soil where first they trod;
They have left unstained what there they found—
　Freedom to worship God!

　　　　　　　　　—Felicia Hemans

123

BREATHES THERE THE MAN

Breathes there the man, with soul so dead,
Who never to himself hath said,
    This is my own, my native land!
Whose heart hath ne'er within him burned,
As home his footsteps he hath turned,
    From wandering on a foreign strand?
If such there breathe, go, mark him well;
For him no minstrel raptures swell;
High though his titles, proud his name,
Boundless his wealth as wish can claim—
Despite those titles, power and pelf,
The wretch, concentered all in self,
Living, shall forfeit fair renown,
And, doubly dying, shall go down
To the vile dust, from whence he sprung,
Unwept, unhonored, and unsung.

—SIR WALTER SCOTT

From THE CENTENNIAL MEDITATION
OF COLUMBIA

Long as thine Art shall love true love,
Long as thy Science truth shall know,
Long as thine Eagle harms no Dove,
Long as thy Law by law shall grow,
Long as thy God is God above,
Thy brother every man below,
So long, dear Land of all my love,
Thy name shall shine, thy fame shall glow!

—SIDNEY LANIER

124

AMERICA'S TASK

With malice toward none;
With charity for all;
With firmness in the right, as God gives us to see the right—
Let us strive on to finish the work we are in:
To bind up the nation's wounds;
To care for him who shall have borne the battle,
   and for his widow and his orphan—
To do all which may achieve and cherish a just and
   lasting peace among ourselves and with all nations.

—ABRAHAM LINCOLN

SONG OF THE UNIVERSAL

And thou, America,
For the scheme's culmination,
Its thought and its reality,
For these (not for thyself)
Thou hast arrived.
Thou, too, surroundest all,
Embracing, carrying, welcoming all;
Thou, too, by pathways broad and new
To the ideal tendest.
The measured faith of other lands,
The grandeur of the past,
Are not for thee.
But grandeurs of thine own,
Deific faiths and amplitude, absorbing,
Comprehending all,
All eligible to all.

—WALT WHITMAN

125

THE NEW COLOSSUS

Not like the brazen giant of Greek fame,
With conquering limbs astride from land to land;
Here at our sea-washed sunset gates shall stand
A mighty woman with a torch, whose flame
Is the imprisoned lightning, and her name,
Mother of exiles. From her beacon hand
Glows world-wide welcome. Her mild eyes command
The air-bridged harbor that twin cities frame.
Keep, ancient lands, your storied pomp, cries she
With silent lips. Give me your tired, your poor,
Your huddled masses yearning to breathe free,
The wretched refuse of your teeming shore,
Send these, the homeless, tempest-tossed, to me:
I lift my lamp beside the golden door.[1]

—EMMA LAZARUS

THE BULWARK OF LIBERTY

What constitutes the bulwark of our own liberty and independ-
ence?
It is not our frowning battlements, our bristling seacoast, our army
and our navy.
Our reliance is in the love of liberty which God has planted in us.
Our defense is in the spirit which prizes liberty as the heritage of
all men in all lands everywhere.
Destroy this spirit, and we have planted the seeds of despotism
at our own doors.

—ABRAHAM LINCOLN

[1] The last five lines are inscribed on the Statue of Liberty in New York
harbor.

126

A NATION'S STRENGTH

What makes a nation's pillars high
 And its foundations strong?
What makes it mighty to defy
 The foes that round it throng?

It is not gold. Its kingdoms grand
 Go down in battle shock;
Its shafts are laid on sinking sand,
 Not on abiding rock.

Is it the sword? Ask the red dust
 Of empires passed away;
The blood has turned their stones to rust,
 Their glory to decay.

And is it pride? Ah, that bright crown
 Has seemed to nations sweet;
But God has struck its luster down
 In ashes at his feet.

Not gold but only men can make
 A people great and strong;
Men who for truth and honor's sake
 Stand fast and suffer long.

Brave men who work while others sleep,
 Who dare while others fly—
They build a nation's pillars deep
 And lift them to the sky.

—RALPH WALDO EMERSON

127

From THE BUILDING OF THE SHIP

Thou, too, sail on, O Ship of State!
Sail on, O UNION, strong and great!
Humanity with all its fears,
With all the hopes of future years,
Is hanging breathless on thy fate!
We know what Master laid thy keel,
What Workmen wrought thy ribs of steel,
Who made each mast, and sail, and rope,
What anvils rang, what hammers beat,
In what a forge and what a heat
Were shaped the anchors of thy hope!
Fear not each sudden sound and shock,
'Tis of the wave and not the rock;
'Tis but the flapping of the sail,
And not a rent made by the gale!
In spite of rock and tempest's roar,
In spite of false lights on the shore,
Sail on, nor fear to breast the sea!
Our hearts, our hopes, are all with thee,
Our hearts, our hopes, our prayers, our tears,
Our faith triumphant o'er our fears,
Are all with thee—are all with thee!

—HENRY WADSWORTH LONGFELLOW

AMERICA'S GOSPEL

Our country hath a gospel of her own
To preach and practice before all the world—
The freedom and divinity of man,
The glorious claims of human brotherhood,
And the soul's fealty to none but God.

—JAMES RUSSELL LOWELL

128

AMERICA'S PROSPERITY

They tell me thou art rich, my country: gold
  In glittering flood has poured into thy chest;
  Thy flocks and herds increase, thy barns are pressed
With harvest, and thy stores can hardly hold
Their merchandise; unending trains are rolled
  Along thy network rails of East and West;
  Thy factories and forges never rest;
Thou art enriched in all things bought and sold!

But dost *thou* prosper? Better news I crave.
  O dearest country, is it well with thee
    Indeed, and is thy soul in health?
A nobler people, hearts more wisely brave,
  And thoughts that lift men up and make them free,—
    These are prosperity and vital wealth!

                              —HENRY VAN DYKE

MY COUNTRY, RIGHT!

        My Country, right!
True to the laws of God and man,
Loyal to justice, fair to life,
Spurning the bigot's spiteful ban,
Holding the world in love's wide span,
Foe of fraternal strife.

        My Country, wrong?
God grant that love may spare that fate;
But, if she errs, God make us wise,
Humbly her faults to contemplate;
Thus may our meekness make her great,
Worthy in Freedom's eyes.

                      —THOMAS CURTIS CLARK

129

From AD PATRIAM

Land of my heart,
What future is before thee? Shall it be
To lie at ease, content with thy bright past,
Heedless of all the world, till idleness
Relax thy limbs, and swoln with wealth and pride
Thou shalt abandon justice and the poor?
Or shalt thou, reawakened, scatter wide
The glorious tidings of a liberty
That lifts the latch of opportunity
First to thy children—then to all mankind?
Love of my soul—God keep thee strong and pure,
That thou shalt be a fitting messenger
To carry hope to all the sons of men.

—WILLIAM DUDLEY FOULKE

THE ERRAND IMPERIOUS

But harken, my America, my own,
　Great Mother with the hill-flower in your hair!
Diviner is that light you bear alone,
　That dream that keeps your face forever fair.

'Tis yours to bear the World-State in your dream;
　To strike down Mammon and his brazen breed;
To build the Brother-Future, beam on beam—
　Yours, mighty one, to shape the mighty deed.

The armèd heavens lean down to hear your fame,
　America: rise to your high-born part:
The thunders of the sea are in your name,
　The splendors of the sunrise in your heart.

—EDWIN MARKHAM

From THE TORCH-BEARERS

America, last hope of man and truth,
  Thy name must through all coming ages be
The badge unspeakable of shame and ruth,
  Or glorious pledge that man through truth is free.
This is thy destiny; the choice is thine
  To lead all nations and outshine them all;
But if thou failest, deeper shame is thine,
  And none shall spare to mock thee in thy fall.

—ARLO BATES

AMERICA PRAYS

Not unto us, not unto us—
  All praise be unto Thee!
For all the gold our coffers hold
  Is Thine, from sea to sea.

Not unto us the glory, Lord,
  For power on sea and land.
Thine be the praise, who set our ways,
  Who guideth with Thy hand.

Not unto us the laurel crown,
  Though name and fame be ours.
Without Thy aid all lowly laid
  Would be our vaunted powers.

Not unto us, not unto us!
  Upon Thy will we wait.
Through all the days Thy name we raise
  Who made our nation great.

—ARTHUR GORDON FIELD

131

THIS IS AMERICA

This is America:
These far-flung prairies, orchard lands,
Mountain heights robed with fir and pine·
Wide plains that feed a starving world
When war's red banner is unfurled;
This God-lent wealth of field and mine;
Proud cities built by eager hands.

This is America:
These factories of fervent toil
And myriad marts of fruitful trade,
With busy streets of hope and zeal;
Fair shrines of art, that serve to heal
All wounds of soul, by conflict made;
Fair churches, built on freedom's soil.

This is America:
Our hope of peace and liberty;
Our dream of equal rights for all.
With no mad threats of tyrant lords,
No need have we of guns and swords.
May no dire fate our dreams befall!
God keep our land forever free!

—THOMAS CURTIS CLARK

AMERICA GREETS AN ALIEN

Hail, guest! We ask not what thou art.
If friend, we greet thee hand and heart;
If stranger, such no longer be;
If foe, our love shall conquer thee.

—AUTHOR UNKNOWN

132

WHAT CONSTITUTES A STATE?

What constitutes a State?
Not high-crown'd battlement or labour'd mound,
    Thick wall or moated gate;
Not cities proud with spires and turrets crown'd;
    Not bays and broad-armed ports
Where, laughing at the storm, rich navies ride;
    Not starred and spangled courts,
Where low-browed baseness wafts perfume to pride;
    No!—men, high-minded men.

        .   .   .   .

    Men who their duties know,
But know their rights, and knowing, dare maintain,
    Prevent the long-aimed blow,
And crush the tyrant while they rend the chain:
    These constitute a State.

—SIR WILLIAM JONES

THE CALL

In days long gone God spake unto our sires:
    "Courage! Launch out! A new world build for me!"
Then to the deep they set their ships, and sailed
    And came to land, and prayed that here might be
A realm from pride and despotism free,
A place of peace, the home of liberty.

Lo, in these days, to all good men and true
    God speaks again: "Launch out upon the deep
And win for me a world of righteousness!"
    Can we, free men, at such an hour still sleep?
O God of Freedom, stir us in our night
That we set forth, for justice, truth and right!

—THOMAS CURTIS CLARK

133

AMERICA FIRST!

Not merely in matters material, but in things of the spirit.

Not merely in science, inventions, motors, and skyscrapers, but also in ideals, principles, character.

Not merely in the calm assumption of rights, but in the glad assumption of duties.

Not flaunting her strength as a giant, but bending in helpfulness over a sick and wounded world like a Good Samaritan.

Not in splendid isolation, but in courageous cooperation.

Not in pride, arrogance, and disdain of other races and peoples, but in sympathy, love, and understanding.

Not in treading again the old, worn, bloody pathway which ends inevitably in chaos and disaster, but in blazing a new trail, along which, please God, other nations will follow, into the New Jerusalem where wars shall be no more.

Some day some nation must take that path—unless we are to lapse once again into utter barbarism—and that honor I covet for my beloved America.

And so, in that spirit and with these hopes, I say with all my heart and soul, "AMERICA FIRST!"

—G. ASHTON OLDHAM

THE LAND WHERE HATE SHOULD DIE

This is the land where hate should die—
    No feuds of faith, no spleen of race,
No darkly brooding fear should try
    Beneath our flag to find a place.
Lo! every people here has sent
    Its sons to answer freedom's call;
Their lifeblood is the strong cement
    That builds and binds the nation's wall.

This is the land where hate should die—
　Though dear to me my faith and shrine,
I serve my country well when I
　Respect beliefs that are not mine.
He little loves his land who'd cast
　Upon his neighbor's word a doubt,
Or cite the wrongs of ages past
　From present rights to bar him out.

This is the land where hate should die—
　This is the land where strife should cease,
Where foul, suspicious fear should fly
　Before our flag of light and peace.
Then let us purge from poisoned thought
　That service to the State we give,
And so be worthy as we ought
　Of this great Land in which we live!
　　　　　　　　　　—Denis A. McCarthy

SERVE IN THY POST

"That humble, simple duty of the day
　Perform," he bids; "ask not if small or great:
Serve in thy post; be faithful and obey;
　Who serves her truly, sometimes serves the State."
　　　　　　　　　　—Arthur Hugh Clough

FOR A PATRIOT

　　　Be just, and fear not:
Let all the ends thou aim'st at be thy country's,
Thy God's, and truth's.
　　　　　　　　　—William Shakespeare
　　　　　　　　　　(Henry VIII)

135

O BEAUTIFUL, MY COUNTRY

O Beautiful, my country!
Be thine a nobler care
Than all thy wealth of commerce,
Thy harvests waving fair:
Be it thy pride to cherish
The manhood of the poor;
Be thou to the oppressèd
Fair Freedom's open door!

For thee our fathers suffered,
For thee they toiled and prayed;
Upon thy holy altar
Their willing lives they laid.
Thou hast no common birthright,
Grand memories on thee shine;
The blood of pilgrim nations
Commingled, flows in thine.

O Beautiful, our country!
Round thee in love we draw;
Thine is the grace of freedom,
The majesty of law.
Be righteousness thy sceptre,
Justice thy diadem;
And on thy shining forehead
Be peace the crowning gem!

—FREDERICK L. HOSMER

Labor Day

STANZAS ON FREEDOM

Men! whose boast it is that ye
Come of fathers brave and free,
If there breathe on earth a slave,
Are ye truly free and brave?
If ye do not feel the chain,
When it works a brother's pain,
Are ye not base slaves indeed,
Slaves unworthy to be freed?

. . . .

Is true Freedom but to break
Fetters for our own dear sake,
And, with leathern hearts, forget
That we owe mankind a debt?
No! true Freedom is to share
All the chains our brothers wear,
And, with heart and hand, to be
Earnest to make others free!

They are slaves who fear to speak
For the fallen and the weak;
They are slaves who will not choose
Hatred, scoffing, and abuse,
Rather than in silence shrink
From the truth they needs must think;
They are slaves who dare not be
In the right with two or three.

—JAMES RUSSELL LOWELL

From THE TOILER

Behold, O world, the Toiling Man,
Bearing earth's burden and her ban.
Because of his all-saving grace,
Kaisers and kings have held their place—
Because he gave ungrudging toil,
The Lords have had the world for spoil—
Because he gave them all his dower,
Great ladies glittered out their hour.
He clothed these paupers, gave them bed,
Put into their mouths their daily bread.
And his reward? A crust to taste,
An unknown grave upon the waste.
Outcast and cursed, befooled and flayed,
With earth's brute burdens on him laid,
He only reached out humble hands,
Reached out his mercies on all lands.
How silent down the world he trod—
How patient he has been with God!

—Edwin Markham

MAN-MAKING

We are all blind until we see
That in the human plan
Nothing is worth the making if
It does not make the man.

Why build these cities glorious
If man unbuilded goes?
In vain we build the work, unless
The builder also grows.

—Edwin Markham

138

CARPENTER CHRIST

Carpenter Christ, I know that you must understand. I praise you
  most for work.
Surely hands that stripped the cedar bough in Nazareth must be
  akin to hands that love the homely touch of bread.
Surely fingers that had no fear to heal the leper must know the
  joy of menial tasks to rest a weary one.
And eyes that watched a passion flower triumphant on a barren
  hill must live again to see the ecstasy of every living bloom.
Carpenter Christ!

—MILDRED FOWLER FIELD

LABOR

We have fed you all for a thousand years,
  And you hail us still unfed,
Though there's never a dollar of all your wealth
  But marks the workers' dead.
We have yielded our best to give you rest,
  And you lie on crimson wool;
For if blood be the price of all your wealth
  Good God, we ha' paid in full!

There's never a mine blown skyward now
  But we're buried alive for you;
There's never a wreck drifts shoreward now
  But we are its ghastly crew;
Go reckon our dead by the forges red,
  And the factories where we spin.
If blood be the price of your cursèd wealth
  Good God, we ha' paid it in!

139

We have fed you all for a thousand years,
   For that was our doom, you know,
From the days when you chained us in your fields
   To the strike of a week ago.
You ha' eaten our lives and our babes and wives,
   And we're told it's your legal share;
But, if blood be the price of your lawful wealth,
   Good God, we ha' bought it fair.

                    —Author Unknown

From A PARABLE

"Have ye founded your thrones and altars, then,
On the bodies and souls of living men?
And think ye that building shall endure,
Which shelters the noble and crushes the poor?

"With gates of silver and bars of gold
Ye have fenced my sheep from their Father's fold;
I have heard the dropping of their tears
In heaven these eighteen hundred years."
  . . . .
Then Christ sought out an artisan,
A low-browed, stunted, haggard man,
And a motherless girl, whose fingers thin
Pushed from her faintly want and sin.

These set he in the midst of them,
And as they drew back their garment-hem,
For fear of defilement, "Lo, here," said he,
"The images ye have made of me!"
                    —James Russell Lowell

THE GLORY OF TOIL

Whether they delve in the buried coal, or plow the upland soil,
Or man the seas, or measure the suns, hail to the men who toil!
It was stress and strain, in wood and cave, while the primal ages
ran
That broadened the brow, and built the brain, and made of a
brute a man;
And better the lot of the sunless mine, the fisher's perilous sea,
Than the slothful ease of him who sleeps in the shade of his bread-
fruit tree;
For sloth is death, and stress is life in all God's realms that are,
And the joy of the limitless heavens is the whirl of star with star!
Still reigns the ancient order—to sow, and reap, and spin;
But oh, the spur of the doing! and oh, the goals to win,
Where each, from the least to the greatest, must bravely bear his
part—
Make straight the furrows, or shape the laws, or dare the crowded
mart!
And he who lays firm the foundations, though strong right arm
may tire,
Is worthy as he who curves the arch, and dreams the airy spire;
For both have reared the minster that shrines the sacred fire.

—EDNA DEAN PROCTOR

From BROTHERHOOD

There shall come from out this noise of strife and groaning
    A broader and a juster brotherhood,
A deep equality of aim, postponing
    All selfish seeking to the general good.
There shall come a time when each shall to another
Be as Christ would have him—brother unto brother.

—SIR LEWIS MORRIS

141

MARY'S SON

Jesus, the friend of lonely, beaten folk,
  Comrade, defender of each humble one,
Who put Your generous shoulders to the yoke
  That we might live in nobler unison,

Why have we worshiped You with sword and flame,
  Placed You, a worker, on a regal throne
And let our brothers' blood flow in Your name
  Who loved all human creatures as Your own?

Let us remember You as Mary's son,
  A worker, seeking rights for men who toil,
Conscious that we are brothers every one
  Upon the glowing earth's fraternal soil.

Let us remember You as one who died
For love of every comrade at his side.

—LUCIA TRENT

BREAD OF BROTHERHOOD

The course of each life must vary
  As the flight of each falling leaf.
For some the journey is lengthened,
  For some the journey is brief.
But praise to the one who travels
  With eyes on the fields of good,
Who makes from each storm-wracked harvest
  The bread of brotherhood.

—LUCIA TRENT

142

RESURGENCE

The Spirit of the Time-to-be,
Of brotherhood, of manhood free,
Spoke to a prostrate world in tears:
"Be not afflicted. Quell thy fears.
Behold the place where oversea—
Europe a charnel house—they laid
And guarded Him. Be not afraid,
For He is risen. Every son
That sees a deed of service done,
A brother's heart by kindness swayed,
Proclaims His resurrection known
Not on a graved tower of piled stone,
But in the every act that can
Bring near the Brotherhood of Man."

—LAURA BELL EVERETT

WORK

Work thou for pleasure.
  Paint or sing or carve
The thing thou lovest,
  Though the body starve.
Who works for glory
  Misses oft the goal,
Who works for money
  Coins his very soul.
Work for the work's sake,
  Then, and it might be
That these things shall
  Be added unto thee.

—KENYON COX

143

From WE ARE THE BURDEN-BEARERS!

We are the Burden-Bearers,
　　We of the bended backs;
We are the shackle-wearers,
　　Stumbling the leaden tracks.

We are the mountain-makers—
　　Steel-girded mountains that rise
Dwarfing the ancient Cheops,
　　Into the city skies.

We are the diggers and delvers
　　Under the river roof,
Tunneling granite highways;
　　We are the warp and the woof.

We are the slaves of traffic
　　Out where the world is new;
We are the scouts of commerce
　　Cutting the pathways through.

We are the naked toilers
　　Fronting the furnace flames;
We are the miracle-makers,
　　Men of the nameless names.
　　．　．　．　．　．　．　．　．　．
We are the stones of the corner;
　　We the foundations of life;
We are the Burden-Bearers
　　Who carry the brunt of the strife!

　　　　　　　　　　—WILLIAM L. STIDGER

THE UNEMPLOYED

In the village squares
In the small parks
In the chaste memorials
We sit and rust,
Veterans of fabulous but forgotten battles,
Unnoticed by bustling shoppers,
By strolling lovers,
By drum majorettes in white boots
And shakos,
Impotent. Usefulness ended,
We are the guns—
Young old men—
Symbols of Peace, now war is ended.

—LeVan Roberts

THE MASTER OF LABORERS

O Master of the common weal,
The shop, the field, the market place!
Thou knowest all the pangs we feel.
Thou knowest all our need of grace;
And where the world's injustice goads
The weary, on the climbing roads,
Stoop once again with tender voice,
Though clanging discord fills the air,
To whisper hope and bid rejoice
All who the world's oppression bear.
O Master of the toiling clan,
Thou Son of God! Thou Son of Man!

—George Edward Day

145

THESE ARE MY PEOPLE

These are my people where bullets fly
And the snorting dragon of death goes by.
Like the faggots he tramples them under claws,
Struggling mice in tomcat paws.

These are my people: the octaroon,
Or white or yellow as harvest moon,
Your people, our people, everyone,
Brothers beneath the beneficent sun,
Brothers through ice or tropic rain,
Brothers in laughter, brothers in pain.

These are my people, yours and mine,
In hobo jungle, by roadway shrine,
In dustbowl fields where the tom-tom sun
Beats all life to oblivion.

Women, whose larders are bare and dry,
Whose withered blossoms of children cry,
Whose husbands curse in the empty room
And scuff their shoes through the dust of doom.

These are my people, I hold them sure
In the brotherhood that shall endure,
In the militant brotherhood that strives
To lift the burden from their lives.

To clothe with sturdy flesh the bone,
To stop the wracking cough and groan,
To fill the stove with coal and wood.
This is the only brotherhood.

146

This is the brotherhood that stirs
Faith where the mammoth engine purrs,
Solidarity where the wheels
Hum a litany that heals,

Hum a ritual that declares
All things come to him who dares,
All things come to those who dare
Unite for plenty everywhere.

These are our people. We hold them sure
In the brotherhood that shall endure,
In the brotherhood that brings to birth
Not slaves but masters of the earth!

—LUCIA TRENT

HISTORY OF THE MODERN WORLD

When men must labor that the wheels may grind,
Then men depend for bread upon the wheels.
So these predominate; their maker kneels,
And sees man's slave the master of mankind.

—STANTON A. COBLENTZ

THE NEW TRINITY

Three things must a man possess if his soul would live,
    And know life's perfect good—
Three things would the all-supplying Father give—
    Bread, Beauty and Brotherhood.

—EDWIN MARKHAM

147

GRATITUDE FOR WORK

Upon thy bended knees, thank God for work—
Work—once man's penance, now his high reward!
For work to do, and strength to do the work,
    We thank Thee, Lord!

Since outcast Adam toiled to make a home,
The primal curse a blessing has become,
Man in his toil finds recompense for loss,
A workless world had known nor Christ nor Cross.

Some toil for love, and some for simple greed,
Some reap a harvest past their utmost need,
More, in their less find truer happiness,
And all, in work, relief from bitterness.

Upon thy bended knees, thank God for work!
In workless days all ills and evils lurk.
For work to do, and strength to do the work,
    We thank Thee, Lord!

            —JOHN OXENHAM

ARISTOCRATS OF LABOR

They claim no guard of heraldry,
    They scorn the knightly rod;
Their coats of arms are noble deeds,
    Their peerage is from God!

            —W. STEWART

148

Columbus Day

COLUMBUS

Behind him lay the gray Azores,
  Behind, the Gates of Hercules;
Before him not the ghost of shores,
  Before him only shoreless seas.
The good mate said: "Now we must pray,
  For lo! the very stars are gone,
Brave Admiral, speak, what shall I say?"
  "Why, say 'Sail on! sail on! and on!'"

"My men grow mutinous day by day;
  My men grow ghastly wan and weak."
The stout mate thought of home; a spray
  Of salt wave washed his swarthy cheek.
"What shall I say, brave Admiral, say,
  If we sight naught but seas at dawn?"
"Why, you shall say at break of day,
  'Sail on! sail on! sail on! and on!'"

They sailed and sailed, as winds might blow,
  Until at last the blanched mate said:
"Why, now not even God would know,
  Should I and all my men fall dead.
These very winds forget their way,
  For God from these dread seas is gone,
Now, speak, brave Admiral, speak and say."
  He said, "Sail on! sail on! and on!"

They sailed. They sailed. Then spoke the mate:
"This mad sea shows his teeth tonight.
He curls his lip, he lies in wait
With lifted teeth, as if to bite!
Brave Admiral, say but one good word:
What shall we do when hope is gone?"
The words leaped like a leaping sword:
"Sail on! sail on! sail on! and on!"

Then pale and worn, he kept his deck,
And peered through darkness. Ah, that night
Of all dark nights! And then a speck—
A light! A light! A light! A light!
It grew, a starlit flag unfurled!
It grew to be Time's burst of dawn.
He gained a world; he gave that world
Its grandest lesson: "On! sail on!"

—Joaquin Miller

THE DISCOVERER

Off from the shore at last he took his way;
Through mist and fog he sailed, in hope and faith;
Day after day he met with curses dire;
Night after night he prayed, and flouting death,
Straight on he held his plain but valiant bark,
Saw cheering visions of his banner furled
On new wide lands. He sought a shorter path
To distant Ind, and here he found—a world.

—Arthur Gordon Field

150

THE PRAYER OF COLUMBUS

One effort more, my altar this bleak sand;
That Thou, O God, my life hast lighted,
With ray of light, steady, ineffable, vouchsafed of Thee,
Light rare untellable, lighting the very light,
Beyond all signs, descriptions, languages;
For that, O God, be it my latest word, here on my knees,
Old, poor, and paralyzed, I thank Thee.

My terminus near,
The clouds already closing in upon me,
The voyage balked, the course disputed, lost,
I yield my ships to Thee.
My hands, my limbs grow nerveless,
My brain feels racked, bewildered,
Let the old timbers part, I will not part,
I will cling fast to Thee, O God, though the waves buffet me,
Thee, Thee at least I know.

— WALT WHITMAN

From CONSCRIPTS OF THE DREAM

Give thanks, O heart, for the high souls
That point us to the deathless goals—
For all the courage of their cry
That echoes down from sky to sky;
Thanksgiving for the armèd seers
And heroes called to mortal years—
Souls that have built our faith in man,
And lit the ages as they ran.

—EDWIN MARKHAM

151

COLUMBUS THE WORLD-GIVER

Who doubts has met defeat ere blows can fall,
Who doubts must die with no palm in his hand;
Who doubts shall never be of that high band
Which clearly answer—Present! to Death's call.
For Faith is life, and, though a funeral pall
Veil our fair Hope, and on our promised land
A mist malignant hang, if Faith but stand
Among our ruins we shall conquer all.

O faithful soul, that knew no doubting low.
O Faith incarnate, lit by Hope's strong flame,
And led by Faith's own cross to dare all ill
And find our world!—but more than this we owe
To thy true heart; thy pure and glorious name
Is one clear trumpet call to Faith and Will.

—MAURICE FRANCIS EGAN

COLUMBUS NEVER KNEW

Columbus never knew that he
    Had won undying fame,
Nor that a thousand places would
    Pay tribute to his name.

Like many men, he could not see
    That failure only seems
The sad conclusion of good work,
    The end of cherished dreams.

Time gave his life a just reward;
    His earnest efforts brought
Acclaim for reaching greater goals
    Than any he had sought.

—GAIL BROOK BURKET

152

From COLUMBUS

One day more
These muttering shoalbrains leave the helm to me.
God, let me not in their dull ooze be stranded;
Let not this one frail bark, to hollow which
I have dug out the pith and sinewy heart
Of my aspiring life's fair trunk, be so
Cast up to warp and blacken in the sun,
Just as the opposing wind 'gins whistle off
His cheek-swollen mates, and from the leaning mast
Fortune's full sail strains forward!
One poor day!—
Remember whose and not how short it is!
It is God's day, it is Columbus's.
A lavish day! One day, with life and heart,
Is more than time enough to find a world.

—JAMES RUSSELL LOWELL

THE DREAMER

Tiring of rest, of plain and fruitless toil,
    He had a dream—of regions wide and free;
That dream was his till, far beyond the seas,
    He found his prize—the Land of Liberty.

—DOROTHY GOULD

153

Armistice—World Order Day

WAR

Hear me, my warriors; my heart is sick and sad;
Our chiefs are killed,
The old men are all dead,
It is cold and we have no blankets;
The little children are freezing to death.
Hear me, my warriors; my heart is sick and sad;
From where the sun now stands I will fight no more forever!
—JOSEPH (a famous Indian chief)

THE NEW MARS

I war against the folly that is War,
  The sacrifice that pity hath not stayed,
The Great Delusion men have perished for,
  The lie that hath the souls of men betrayed:
I war for justice and for human right,
Against the lawless tyranny of might.

A monstrous cult has held the world too long:
  The worship of a Moloch that hath slain
Remorselessly the young, the brave, the strong—
  Indifferent to the unmeasured pain,
The accumulated horror and despair,
That stricken Earth no longer wills to bear.

154

My goal is *peace*—not peace at any price,
  While yet ensanguined jaws of evil yawn
Hungry and pitiless: Nay, peace were vice
  Until the cruel dragon-teeth be drawn,
And the wronged victims of oppression be
Delivered from its hateful rule and free!

When comes that hour, resentment laid aside,
  Into a ploughshare will I beat my sword;
The weaker nations' strength shall be my pride,
  Their gladness my exceeding great reward;
And not in vain shall be the tears now shed,
Nor vain the service of the gallant dead.

I war against the folly that is War,
  The futile sacrifice that nought hath stayed,
The Great Delusion men have perished for,
  The lie that hath the souls of men betrayed:
For faith I war, humanity and trust;
For peace on earth—a lasting peace, and just!
                    —FLORENCE EARLE COATES

APPARITIONS

Who goes there, in the night,
  Across the storm-swept plain?
We are the ghosts of a valiant war—
  A million murdered men!

Who goes there, at the dawn,
  Across the sun-swept plain?
We are the hosts of those who swear:
  It shall not be again!
                    —THOMAS CURTIS CLARK

155

A SERGEANT'S PRAYER

Almighty and all present Power,
Short is the prayer I make to Thee,
I do not ask in battle hour
For any shield to cover me.

The vast unalterable way,
From which the stars do not depart
May not be turned aside to stay
The bullet flying to my heart.

I ask no help to strike my foe,
I ask no petty victory here,
The enemy I hate, I know,
To Thee is also dear.

But this I pray, be at my side
When death is drawing through the sky,
Almighty God who also died
Teach me the way that I should die.

—HUGH BRODIE

PEACE

O brother, lift a cry, a long world cry
Sounding from sky to sky—
The cry of one great word,
Peace, peace, the world will clamoring to be heard—
A cry to break the ancient battle-ban,
To end it in the sacred name of Man!

—EDWIN MARKHAM

VIA DOLOROSA

They marched,
That sun-gold summer day,
Their hard young bodies stiff in olive drab,
Their eyes seeing a new world
Safe for a race of dreamers,
While we who watched
Shouted with the band,
"Over there,"
"When you come back—for you will come back—"
Even, "Mine eyes have seen the glory."
God forbid!
How could our eyes have failed to see
The crutches and the empty sleeves,
The groping canes, the useless hands,
The gruesome masks?

Forgive us that we did not see
The other regiment that marched that day,
And You there among them,
Staggering with the cross.

—PHOEBE SMITH

DISARM THE HEARTS

In hearts too young for enmity there lies the way
    to make men free;
When children's friendships are world wide
New ages will be glorified.
Let child love child, and strife will cease.
Disarm the hearts, for that is peace.

—ETHEL BLAIR JORDAN

157

THE HYMN OF HATE

And this I hate—not men, nor flag, nor race,
But only War with its wild, grinning face.
God strike it till its eyes be blind as night
And all its members tremble with affright!
Oh, let it hear in its death agony
The wail of mothers for their best-loved ones,
   And on its head
Descend the venomed curses of the sons
Who followed it, deluded, where its guns
   Had dyed the daisies red.

All these I hate—war and its panoply,
The lie that hides its ghastly mockery,
That makes its glories out of women's tears,
The toil of peasants through the burdened years,
The legacy of long disease that preys
On bone and body in the afterdays.
   God's curses pour,
Until it shrivel with its votaries
And die away in its own fiery seas,
   That nevermore
Its dreadful call of murder may be heard;
A thing accursed in very deed and word
   From blood-drenched shore to shore!
     —Joseph Dana Miller

DANGER

O foolish builders!
Not as the Architect Eternal planned,
Ye think with frame of steel to make it stand—
House of the Future, built upon the sand.
     Theodora L. Paine

158

THE DAY

Not as they planned it or will plan again,
Those captains whose commands were forged in hell,
Not as they promised for their terrible
Obedient horde, Teuton and Saracen,
Bulgar and Slav, not as they dreamed it then,
Masters of might with sobs for paeans to swell
Their darkening way, but like a far-off bell
Undoing night—the day has come for men.

The people's day has dawned, a deeper sky
Than any day that ever rose from sea,
And more than any captain dared is won,
And this great light that opens carries high
More justice than we dreamed of, even we
Who are still blind a while, facing the sun.

—WITTER BYNNER

From DISARMAMENT

"Put up the sword!" The voice of Christ once more
Speaks, in the pauses of the cannon's roar,
O'er fields of corn by fiery sickles reaped
And left dry ashes; over trenches heaped
With nameless dead; o'er cities starving slow
Under a rain of fire; through wards of woe
Down which a groaning diapason runs
From tortured brothers, husbands, lovers, sons
Of desolate women in their far-off homes,
Waiting to hear the step that never comes!
O men and brothers! let that voice be heard.
War fails, try peace; put up the useless sword!

—JOHN GREENLEAF WHITTIER

159

DESIGN FOR PEACE

How shall the bayonet and bomb
Of war bring the millennium?
And how shall nations that draw food
From earth so saturate with blood
Sustain the liberty they save?
A world has pressed into the grave
Its young, the beautiful and brave.

Lord of our strength, and the vast source
Of war and peace in moving course,
Ruler of earth and universe,
Lift from each soul his ancient curse:
The cruel thought, the lying word,
The grasping hand, the vengeful sword.

Grant victory, to every man his part,
The battleline is drawn in every heart!
—JANET NORRIS BANGS

PEACE ON EARTH

Peace, peace on earth! the heart of man forever
    Through all these weary strifes foretells the day;
Blessed be God, the hope forsakes him never,
    That war shall end and swords be sheathed for aye.

Peace, peace on earth! for men shall love each other,
    Host shall go forth to bless and not destroy;
For man shall see in every man a brother,
    And peace on earth fulfill the angels' joy.
—SAMUEL LONGFELLOW

GREAT POWERS CONFERENCE

The blind men add the figures, draw the maps.
   The deaf men blow the bugles, beat the drums.
And peace becomes a wavering perhaps,
   And war a tidal wave that goes and comes.

The legless men march forward to success.
   The armless men cry: "Victory within reach!"
And life becomes a length of more or less,
   With sure uncertainty for all and each.

The men without a heart dispense relief,
   The mindless men devise a master plan.
The perfect government ensues, in brief,
   The Commonwealth of Man without the man.
                  —EDITH LOVEJOY PIERCE

THE WASTE OF WAR

This the law of all war through all ages:
   The choice of the earth it will claim;
It is writ on a thousand red pages:
   "We call not your weak and your lame!"

The fruit of your home you must send us!
   You, mother, the strongest you bore!
The blood-mark is there on your gatepost,
   The Herod of hate and of war!

Your red-blooded, high-browed, heroic!
   The clear-eyed, alert of your sons;
The mighty of muscle, the lithe-limbed;
   The clear-thinking, keen-minded ones!

161

So—build you a race on the weaklings;
  The cycle of growth starts again;
Go back to the place where you struggled,
  And travail a new birth of men!

This the law of all war through all ages:
  The choice of the earth it will claim;
It is writ on a thousand red pages:
  "We call not your weak and your lame!"
                              —WILLIAM L. STIDGER

WHICH SWORD?

A sword, a sword, and a sword;
  Which sword will you draw, my Son?
For one is of steel with its blind appeal
  Till the folly of war is done.
'Tis an honor to fight for God and the right
  But justice is seldom won.

And one is the sword of truth,
  God's swift and naked blade
That puts to flight the lies of night
  And the hatred falsehoods made.
We are cowards all when lies appall,
  But in truth we are unafraid.

And one is a flaming sword
  Whose work is just begun;
Its glorious part is to change the heart,
  Its victories always won.
Draw this and smite with all thy might—
  'Tis the sword of love, my Son.
                              —JASON NOBLE PIERCE

162

ARMISTICE

We face the nations with one hand outstretched
In greeting, and with peace upon our lips;
But in our hearts a question, in our minds
The haunting echoes of the song of war,
The song that sets the world a-tremble still
And shakes the very pillars of our faith.

How long before the peace can pass our lips,
Can claim our minds and drive out old distrust?
To doubt mankind is but to doubt ourselves.
When shall our fingers dare to drop the sword,
While with unquestioning eyes we reach two hands
In open comradeship to all the world?
       —Eunice Mitchell Lehmer

THIS IS THE LAST

Coming in splendor through the golden gate
Of all the days, swift passing, one by one,
O silent planet, thou hast gazed upon
How many harvestings dispassionate?
Across the many-furrowed fields of Fate,
Wrapt in the mantle of oblivion,
The old, gray, wrinkled Husbandman has gone;
The blare of trumpets, rattle of the drum,
Disturb him not at all—he sees,
Between the hedges of the centuries,
A thousand phantom armies go and come,
While reason whispers as each marches past,
"This is the last of wars—this is the last!"
       —Gilbert Waterhouse

163

From THE BOOK OF THE PEOPLE

Your task is to form the universal family, to build the City of God, and by a continuous labor gradually to translate his work in humanity into fact.

When you love one another as brothers, and treat each other reciprocally as such; when each one, seeking his own good in the good of all, shall identify his own life with the life of all, his own interests with the interests of all, and shall be always ready to sacrifice himself for all the members of the human family—then most of the ills which weigh upon the human race will vanish, as thick mists gathered upon the horizon vanish at the rising of the sun.

—ROBERT DE LAMENNAIS

MAKE WAY!

The crashing sky has swept old paths aside.
Old landmarks gone. Old bridges ground to dust.
The ferment, red with the defeating rust
Of spent illusions, bears no friendly guide.
No arrow of tradition points the turn.
In all the wilderness no voice calls "Come!"
This is the desolation and the sum
Of all defeat. The ash spilled from the urn.

Yet, here in this black death, bitter to taste,
Out of the surging slime—a new design—
The substance fitted into better line
And form. The matrix purged of clogging waste.
Make way! Make way! From scourging pain shall rise
The flame that lights the candles in men's eyes.

—FLORENCE CROCKER COMFORT

PREPAREDNESS

One weapon I would keep
From the world's scrapheap
Of longbows and swords,
Of bayonets and guns—
One weapon for my soul's defense.

Leave me the sword of truth,
Swift and sharp and strong
To pierce the subtle lie
In militant word and song—
One weapon for this land's defense.

Throw all else on the scrapheap.
Only one weapon let us keep.

—JEAN GRIGSBY PAXTON

ARCHITECTS OF DREAM

We cannot rest, whose hearts are like the breakers
    That pound forever in rebellious moan.
We cannot rest, who are the bright awakers,
    The trumpeters that mock the tyrants' throne.

We are the architects of dream, who cherish
    A beauty others never learned to feel.
The towers that we build shall never perish,
    For they are reared of spirit, not of steel.

We cannot rest, whose tongues are quick with pity
    For those who ply the ponderous wheels of toil,
The builders of the unsurrendering city,
    To stand upon the new fraternal soil.

—LUCIA TRENT

165

"NEXT TIME"

The order goes; what if we rush ahead
  With friendly shouts, with welcoming and cheer
And loyal clasp of fellowship—instead
  Of lethal gas, and bombs that maim and sear—
    "Next time"?

If, in accord, the armies look afar
  Where droops a Figure on a Cross; and hear,
"Of all my woe, ye make a mockery!"
  With Him allied, what cause have we to fear—
    "Next time"?

Firm in our faith, we stand together there,
  Comrades and brothers; if we must be slain
So let our captains take us; but beware!
  They cannot make us ope His wounds again—
    "Next time"!

—LAURA SIMMONS

VICTORY PARADE

Cruisers, destroyers, carriers align
For a great show of force at victory's sign.
Far lands acknowledge our increased domain
And hail us leaders of the nations' train.

Power and showy pride—can these replace
The radiance of innocence and grace?
The imperative of penitential tears?
And freedom from our vast ambitions' fears?

—GEORGE EDWARD HOFFMAN

SONG FOR TOMORROW

O children of men, O sons and daughters of sorrow,
Raise your bewildered eyes to the luminous hills of tomorrow!
Look at your feet, at the orgy of hideous plunder.
See how the poor and the needy are trampled brutally under!

Yet out of your mad machinery, your arrogant motors whirring,
Something triumphant and brave and beautiful will be stirring.
Out of the futile murder in thousands of jails and in battle,
Out of your greed and all your vain hypocritical prattle,

A courage will rise and a faith in comradely giving
That will lead your turbulent feet to the City of Brotherly
    Living.
O children of men, O sons and daughters of sorrow,
Raise your bewildered eyes to the luminous hills of tomorrow.
                                                —LUCIA TRENT

LITANY FOR PEACE

No longer homes are flame against
A lurid sky; the ash is gray
Where men have warred.
But through the dark a jackal cries,
The wolves of hate and hunger stalk—
Have mercy, Lord!

Across wide seas the children's sobs
Sound faint and far. War-worn,
We sheathe the sword;
Lest we neglect a torch to light
Our brethren groping through the night,
Be with us, Lord!
                                        —LESLIE SAVAGE CLARK

167

THE VALLEY OF DECISION

The World is in the Valley of Decision;
    It is standing at the parting of the ways;
Will it climb the steps of God to realm elysian—
Or fall on horror of still darker days?

Will it free itself of every shameful shackle?
    Will it claim the glorious freedom of the brave?
Will it lose the soul of Life in this debacle,
    And sink into a mean dishonored grave?

All the world is in the Valley of Decision,
    And out of it there is but one sure road;
Eyes unsealed can still foresee the mighty vision
    Of a world in travail turning unto God.

All the world is in the Valley of Decision.
    Who shall dare its future destiny foretell?
Will it yield its soul unto the Heavenly Vision,
    Or sink despairing into its own hell?

—JOHN OXENHAM

TRUE FREEDOM

'Tis not in blood that Liberty inscribes her civil laws,
She writes them on the people's hearts in language clear and plain;
True thoughts have moved the world before, and so they shall
    again.
We yield to none in earnest love of freedom's cause sublime;
We join the cry "Fraternity!" We keep the march of Time.

—CHARLES MACKAY

NO ARMISTICE IN LOVE'S WAR

What are poets? Are they only drums commanding?
  Trumpets snarling, moving men to hate and ravage?
Were their songs of war the snares of Trade demanding
  Lives, and binding men to gods senile and savage?

What are soldiers? Only power, to be broken
  On the wheels of Business when there is no battle?
"War to end war," was that but falsely spoken?
  Whom has war set free? Have rifles stopped their
    rattle?

Many suffer hunger while the few still plunder.
  Dreams of peace and brotherhood are all undone.
Let poets' songs boom loud with love's own battle
    thunder!
  War has ended? No, the war has just begun.

—RALPH CHEYNEY

From LET US DECLARE!

Come, workers! Poets, artists, dreamers, more and more
Let us shake out our wings and soar.
Let us not fear to answer the high call
That trumpets to us all.
Amid the doubts and chaos of today—
The hate, the lust, the rage,
Let us declare for nobler things—
The coming of that age
When man shall find his wings!

—ANGELA MORGAN

169

LESSONS

Strange lesson taught by war
  Is this, its legacy:
Wrecked homes, bare fields, sick hearts
  And thwarted destiny.

Stranger still the lesson
  If brotherhood increase
In ratio to our hunger—
  Hunger for bread and peace.

—HELEN WEBER

LET DREAMERS WAKE

Now, if ever, let poets sing,
  Now, if ever, let dreamers wake;
Now, let the Bearers of Beauty bring
  Light where the patterns of madness break.
You who are gifted with tongues of fire,
  In whose lonely bosoms the Word lies lost—
The Word that answers the world's desire—
  Speak it boldly, nor count the cost.
Carve it on altar and steel and stone;
  Write it in flame on the darkened sky;
Shout it over the bomber's drone—
  Whisper it softly where heroes die.
Now, to keep silence is treason's part;
  Sing till the voices of greed are dumb;
Dip your pen in the people's heart—
  Chart the tides of millennium!

—LILITH LORRAINE

CHALLENGE

This is no time for fear, for doubts of good,
For broodings on the tragedies of fate.
It is a time for songs of brotherhood,
For hymns of joy, of man's divine estate.
Though echoes of old wars depress the heart,
Though greed and hate still curse men's nobler ways,
Though strife and tumult blast our life apart,
It is a time for confidence and praise.
Let prophets prophesy, let poets sing.
Our dreams are not in vain. The night is past.
Together, as new hopes are wakening,
Let us proclaim, The Kingdom comes at last!
Our Babels crash. Let selfish flags be furled.
As brothers all, we build a Friendly World.

—THOMAS CURTIS CLARK

THE DREAMERS CRY THEIR DREAM

The dreamers upon the hilltops
    Catch visions that flame the mind.
They call the shackled plainsmen
    To leave their hills behind.

But the plainsmen keep on plodding
    And the dreamers cry their dream
And now and then a plainsman
    Catches tomorrow's gleam.

The dreamers still cry their heart-song.
    Their citadels never fade.
Some day mankind will be claiming
    The world the dreamers made.

—LUCIA TRENT

171

ARMISTICE DAY VOW

Our millions rose in arms, one fateful day,
To meet a giant foe. They fought full well,
And as from demon ships the grim bombs fell,
They won their fight. And is there more to tell?

Ah, yes! Their sacrifice is all in vain
Unless we, saved from death by their brave fight
For lasting peace, now stand forth in our might
For truth and justice, and God's valiant right!

—DOROTHY GOULD

From LOCKSLEY HALL

For I dipped into the future, far as human eye could see,
Saw the Vision of the world, and all the wonder that would be;

Saw the heavens fill with commerce, argosies of magic sails,
Pilot of the purple twilight, dropping down with costly bales;

Heard the heavens fill with shouting, and there rained a ghastly
dew
From the nations' airy navies grappling in the central blue;

Far along the world-wide whisper of the south-wind rushing warm,
With the standards of the peoples plunging through the thunder-
storm;

Till the war-drum throbbed no longer, and the battle-flags were
furled
In the Parliament of Man, the Federation of the world.

—ALFRED TENNYSON

172

THE TOURNAMENT OF MAN

Clear the field for the grand tournament of the nations!
The struggle to think the best thought, and to express
it, in tone and color and form and word;
The struggle to do the greatest deeds, and lead the no-
blest and most useful lives;
The struggle to see clearest and know truest and love
strongest.
Your other blood-and-bludgeon contests but postpone
the real fray.
The true knights are yearning to enter the lists, and
you block the high festival with your brawling.
Is it possible you mistake this for the real event of
history?
Away with your brutal disorder, and clear the field for
the tournament of Man.

—Ernest Crosby

THE GOAL AND THE WAY

The future lies
With those whose eyes
    Are wide to the necessities,
And wider still
With fervent will
    To all the possibilities.

Times big with fate
Our wills await,
    If we be ripe to occupy;
If we be bold
To seize and hold
    This new-born liberty.

173

And every man
Not only can
    But *must* the great occasion seize.
Never again
Will he attain
    Such wondrous opportunities.

Be strong! Be true!
Claim your soul's due!
    Let no men rob you of the prize!
The goal is near,
The way is clear,
    Who falters now shames God, and dies.
                —JOHN OXENHAM

BROTHERHOOD

The crest and crowning of all good,
Life's final star is Brotherhood;
For it will bring again to Earth
Her long-lost Poesy and Mirth,
Will send new light on every face,
A kingly power upon the race,
And till it comes, we men are slaves,
And travel downward to the dust of graves.

Come, clear the way then, clear the way:
Blind creeds and kings have had their day.
Break the dead branches from the path:
Our hope is in the aftermath—
Our hope is in heroic men,
Star-led to build the world again.
To this Event the ages ran:
Make way for Brotherhood—make way for Man.
                —EDWIN MARKHAM

THE NEW SONG

Poet, take up your lyre;
No more shall warlike fire
    Inflame the earth and sea;
Cease from your martial strain,
Sing songs of peace again,
    Sing of a world set free.

No more sing fear and hate
While armies devastate,
    Nor boast of foes withstood;
Let mercy be your theme,
Renew the old, fair dream
    Of human brotherhood.

No more the trumpet blast
Shall call to conflict fast,
    The flame of war grows pale;
Sing, Poet, God-inspired,
Till all the world is fired
    With love that shall not fail.
                    —ARTHUR GORDON FIELD

THE MESSAGE OF PEACE

Bid the din of battle cease!
    Folded be the wings of fire!
Let your courage conquer peace—
    Every gentle heart's desire.

Let the crimson flood retreat!
    Blended in the arc of love.
Let the flags of nations meet;
    Bind the raven, loose the dove;

At the altar that we raise
  King and Kaiser may bow down;
Warrior-Knights above their bays
  Wear the sacred olive crown.

Blinding passion is subdued,
  Men discern their common birth,
God hath made of kindred blood
  All the peoples of the earth.

High and holy are the gifts
  He has lavished on the race—
Hope that quickens, prayer that lifts,
  Honor's meed, and beauty's grace.

As in Heaven's bright face we look
  Let our kindling souls expand;
Let us pledge, on nature's book,
  Heart to heart and hand to hand.

For the glory that we saw
  In the battle-flag unfurled,
Let us read Christ's better law;
  Fellowship for all the world!
                —JULIA WARD HOWE

THE UNIVERSAL REPUBLIC

Upon the skyline i' the dark
The Sun that now is but a spark;
  But soon will be unfurled
The glorious banner of us all,
The flag that rises ne'er to fall,
  Republic of the World!
                —VICTOR HUGO

176

A NEW PATRIOTISM

We need a new patriotism,
A patriotism of unselfishness,
Of impartial good will;
A patriotism that loves other nations
As we love our own.

We need a far-seeing patriotism
That will look beyond the deeds of today
To the consequences of tomorrow;
A patriotism that can envision universal Commonweal.

We need an all-inclusive patriotism
Of practical unity,
Of co-operation,
Of active brotherhood,
As wide as the world
And as deep as the Kingdom of God.

—CHAUNCEY R. PIETY

From THE ARSENAL AT SPRINGFIELD

Were half the power, that fills the world with terror,
    Were half the wealth, bestowed on camps and courts,
Given to redeem the human mind from error,
    There were no need of arsenals or forts;

The warrior's name would be a name abhorrèd!
    And every nation, that should lift again
Its hand against a brother, on its forehead
    Would wear forevermore the curse of Cain!

Down the dark future, through long generations,
    The echoing sounds grow fainter and then cease;
And like a bell, with solemn, sweet vibrations,
    I hear once more the voice of Christ say, "Peace!"

Peace! and no longer from its brazen portals
    The blast of War's great organ shakes the skies!
But beautiful as songs of the immortals,
    The holy melodies of love arise.
                    —HENRY WADSWORTH LONGFELLOW

WILD WEATHER

A great wind sweeps
Across the world, hurling to heaps
Of gilded rubbish crowns and thrones, mere gleam
And flicker of dry leaves in its fierce path,
A wind whose very wrath
Springs from white Alpine crests of thought and dream.

What sword can quell
An unleashed tempest, and compel
Hush to the thunder, patience to the storm?
The maddened blast that buffets sea and land
Blows under high command,
Rending and riving only to transform.

May its wild wings
Burst the old tanglement of things,
Those withered vines and brambles that enmesh
The leaping foot! May its rough flail destroy
Hedges that limit joy,
Leaving, like rain, a silvery earth and fresh!

178

Faith shall not quail
For broken branches of the gale.
Time is a strong corrival and will win.
When hurricane has done its dread behest,
And forests are at rest,
His quiet hand will lead the sunshine in.

— Katharine Lee Bates

BLOW, BUGLE!

Blow, bugle!
But call us not again to battle.
Blow, blow, but waste no mortal's breath
In summoning our lads to death.
No more shall they be driven cattle!
Their war, and ours, is now for life.

Blow, bugle!
Predict the dawn, a friendly world—
For peace our labors!
Blow valiantly, to stay our hopes.
Blow, blow, though mankind blindly gropes.
All lands shall yet be friends and neighbors.
Today, let battle flags be furled.

Blow, bugle!
The world, repentant, longs for peace,
And needs your cheering.
Blow, bugle, lift a heavenly strain
That shall bring hope to life again.
Blow, as that sun-crowned day is nearing
When war and strife at last shall cease.

—Thomas Curtis Clark

WITHOUT REGRET

This is the day the prophets have foretold,
    This is the hour for which the Chosen wait,
This is the requiem of the Age of Gold,
    This is the end of Babylon the Great.
May we who write the annals of this hour
    Suspend our pens in silence, speak no word
Of greed that blossomed like an evil flower,
    Of peace that perished crucified, unheard.

Write only for a cleaner, kindlier race
    After the last bomb thunders from the skies,
That love survived the Terror out of Space,
    And that the Grass is infinitely wise.
Yes, grass is merciful—without regret,
And what it covers . . . let all men forget.
                            —LILITH LORRAINE

WHERE ARE YOU GOING, GREAT-HEART?

    Where are you going, Great-Heart,
    With your eager face and your fiery grace?
    Where are you going, Great-Heart?

    "To fight a fight with all my might;
    For Truth and Justice, God and Right;
    To grace all Life and His fair Light."
        Then God go with you, Great-Heart!

    Where are you going, Great-Heart?
    "To live Today above the Past;
    To make Tomorrow sure and fast;
    To nail God's colors to the mast."
        Then God go with you, Great-Heart!

180

Where are you going, Great-Heart?
"To break down old dividing lines;
To carry out my Lord's designs;
To build again His broken shrines."
    Then God go with you, Great-Heart!

Where are you going, Great-Heart?
"To set all burdened peoples free;
To win for all God's liberty;
To 'stablish His Sweet Sovereignty."
    God goeth with you, Great-Heart!
        —JOHN OXENHAM

THERE IS YET TIME

    This first year
    Of the atom,
    Man of earth,
    Mark the cross
    Upon your brow.
    Dust of Hiroshima,
    Sear the soul
    To repentance.
    There is yet time.
        —ARVEL STEECE

ARMISTICE DAY

Let us evoke no phantom throng
With marble monument and song,
With mock solemnity that comes
From marching feet and muffled drums.

181

But in this drift of after years
Let us pay honor with our tears.
They dared to die, let us who live
Dare to have pity and forgive.

—LUCIA TRENT

WORLD PLANNERS

The world planners gather.
The young men mixed red blood with blue water
And windy sands covered shattered helmets.
The old men confer with figures
And refashion their empires.
They seek a solution; they have it,
And they know it not.

Once when the world was younger
Some nineteen hundred years,
A quiet man walked the Judean hills
And along Galilee's shore,
Then men left their nets.
And he spoke to the people
On a mountain with loaves and fishes,
And he entered the city on a burro,
And they hailed him emperor—
And they nailed him to a cross.
"The Kingdom of God is among you."
They worshiped his teaching
But were afraid to live it.

The world planners gather,
They seek a solution; they have it,
And they know it not.

—ARVEL STEECE

WE WHO BUILD VISIONS

Stalled on the sidelines we must hope and wait,
We who build visions of a world at peace.
We cannot bid the cindery storms to cease,
Nor halt the flame-winds of men's rage and hate.
Nor can we dream that pens will legislate
Or the heart check the sword while swords increase,
Nor that our sobs or prayers will earn release
From those blood-spotted hands that desecrate.

Yet this we know: the world is peace at heart.
With peace the woods are green; the stars recite
Her wordless litanies; and in the soul
Of the strong hills she plays a timeless part,
And in man's spirit, where she comes by night
And shall remain when the last gunfires roll.

—STANTON A. COBLENTZ

PREPARE

O human hearts,
    Beating through fear, through jealousy,
    Through pride, through avarice, through
      bitterness,
Through agony, through death.
    Beating, beating,
    Shame and forgiveness,
    Bewilderment and love,
O my own country,
    My new world,
    Prepare,
    Prepare—
Not to avenge wrong

183

But to exalt right,
Not to display honor
But to prove humility,
Not to bring wrath
    But vision,
Not to win war
    But a people,
And not people only,
But all peoples,.
Not to exact justice from your enemies only
    But from your friends,
And not from your friends only
    But first from yourselves!

—WITTER BYNNER

VICTORY

Beware, beware the snare of "victory."
That they are slaves
The vanquished are well aware;
But, ah! No less are they that call themselves
"The victors."
Stand up! Dare now admit
We too are fools and knaves.

—ROGER AXFORD

Thanksgiving Day

From A TE DEUM OF THE COMMONPLACE

For all the wonders of this wondrous world:
The pure pearl splendors of the coming day,
The breaking east—the rosy flush—the dawn,
For that bright gem in morning's coronal,
That one lone star that gleams above the glow;
For that high glory of the impartial sun—
The golden noonings big with promised life;
The matchless pageant of the evening skies,
The wide-flung gates—the gleams of Paradise,
Supremest visions of Thine artistry;
The sweet, soft gloaming, and the friendly stars;
The vesper stillness, and the creeping shades;
The moon's pale majesty, the pulsing dome,
Wherein we feel Thy great heart throbbing near;
For sweet laborious days and restful nights;
For work to do, and strength to do the work—
      We thank Thee, Lord!

                          —JOHN OXENHAM

THANKSGIVING

Heap high the board with plenteous cheer and gather to the feast,
And toast that sturdy Pilgrim band whose courage never ceased.
Give praise to that All-Gracious One by whom their steps were led,
And thanks unto the harvest's Lord who sends our daily bread.
                    —ALICE WILLIAMS BROTHERTON

From FOR AN AUTUMN FESTIVAL

Once more the liberal year laughs out
   O'er richer stores than gems or gold;
Once more with harvest-song and shout
   Is Nature's bloodless triumph told.

. . . .

O favors every year made new!
   O gifts with rain and sunshine sent!
The bounty overruns our due,
   The fulness shames our discontent.

We shut our eyes, the flowers bloom on;
   We murmur, but the corn-ears fill;
We choose the shadow, but the sun
   That casts it shines behind us still.

. . . .

Who murmurs at his lot to-day?
   Who scorns his native fruit and bloom?
Or sighs for dainties far away,
   Beside the bounteous board of home?

Thank Heaven, instead, that Freedom's arm
   Can change a rocky soil to gold—
That brave and generous lives can warm
   A clime with northern ices cold.

And let these altars, wreathed with flowers
   And piled with fruits, awake again
Thanksgivings for the golden hours,
   The early and the latter rain!

            —JOHN GREENLEAF WHITTIER

186

THANKSGIVING

What art Thou saying, Lord, to me
By the red-fruited tree—
The yellow pumpkin on its frosted vine—
The purple grapes down by the old stone wall—
That tangle of late asters—silken corn-stalks tall—
Beauty of naked branches and a saffron sky,
That squadron of wild geese that southward fly?
Even the humble carrot hath an orange coat,
The beet a crimson robe—an onion silver skin.
By the rich walnut tree
I see the grey squirrel scampering, filling winter-bin.
The dainty weed beside the road doth yield
A perfect seed, wrought with divinest care;
Sometimes the wonder seems too great to bear.
O Lord, Thy beauteous bounty doth ensnare my soul!
I bow with great thanksgiving!

—GENE H. OSBORNE

THANK GOD FOR LIFE

Thank God for life; life is not sweet always.
Hands may be heavy laden, heart care-full;
Unwelcome nights follow unwelcome days,
And dreams divine end in awakenings dull;
Still it is life; and life is cause for praise.
This ache, this restlessness, this quickening sting
Prove me no torpid and inanimate thing—
Prove me of Him who is the life, the spring.
I am alive—and that is beautiful.

—AUTHOR UNKNOWN

WE THANK THEE!

For glowing autumn's brimming yield,
The rich returns of wood and field,
For well-filled bins and orchard gold—
Earth's harvest boons are manifold.

For these we thank Thee, Lord of all;
No other Name today we call.
Turn Thou our hearts from thoughts of greed
As from Thy kindly hand we feed.

For this we thank Thee—autumn's gain;
But may we not those gifts disdain
The striving centuries have brought:
The gift of freedom, conflict-bought;

The faith in God our fathers passed
To us in turn. May we hold fast
To all these treasures of our sires;
May we not scorn their altar-fires!

We thank Thee: Thou hast brought us good
From hill and prairie, field and wood.
We thank Thee: Teach us how to pray
"Our Father" on this festal day.
                              —THOMAS CURTIS CLARK

THANKSLIVING

Were thanks with every gift expressed,
    Each day would be Thanksgiving;
Were gratitude its very best,
    Each life would be thanksliving.
                              —CHAUNCEY R. PIETY

THANKS BE TO GOD

I do not thank Thee, Lord,
That I have bread to eat while others starve;
Nor yet for work to do
While empty hands solicit Heaven;
Nor for a body strong
While other bodies flatten beds of pain.
No, not for these do I give thanks!

But I am grateful, Lord,
Because my meager loaf I may divide;
For that my busy hands
May move to meet another's need;
Because my doubled strength
I may expend to steady one who faints.
Yes, for all these do I give thanks!

For heart to share, desire to bear
And will to lift,
Flamed into one by deathless Love—
Thanks be to God for this!
Unspeakable! His Gift!

—JANIE ALFORD

OUR PRAYER

Thou that hast given so much to me,
Give one thing more—a grateful heart;
Not thankful when it pleaseth me,
As if Thy blessings had spare days;
But such a heart, whose pulse may be
Thy praise.

—GEORGE HERBERT

189

WE THANK THEE

Not for our lands, our wide-flung prairie wealth,
    Our mighty rivers born of friendly spring,
Our inland seas, our mountains proud and high,
    Forests and orchards richly blossoming;
Not for these, Lord, our deepest thanks are said
    As, humbly glad, we hail this day serene;
Not for these most, dear Father of our lives,
    But for the love that in all things is seen.

. . . .

We thank Thee, Lord, on this recurring day,
    For liberty to worship as we will;
We thank Thee for the hero souls of old
    Who dared wild seas their mission to fulfill.
O, gird our hearts with stalwart faith in good,
    Give us new trust in Thy providing hand,
And may a spirit born of brotherhood
    Inspire our hearts and bless our native land.

                  —THOMAS CURTIS CLARK

PRAYER

Keep me from fretting, Lord, today
    About my lightened purse;
An empty soul, an empty mind
    Are infinitely worse.
Keep me from dwelling, Lord, I pray,
    Upon tomorrow's bread;
But grant my brother's need shall find
    I thought of him instead.

                  —MAY CARLETON LORD

190

YOUTH'S THANKFULNESS

We lift our glad hearts, Lord, in thankfulness,
  Upon our knees we humbly give Thee praise
For all the harvestings that richly bless
  And strengthen us to battle with the days;
The ruddy apples gathered from the trees,
  The moon-faced pumpkins smiling through the dusk,
The honey freighted homeward by the bees,
  The corn and wheat now wrested from the husk.

But most of all we thank Thee, Lord, for dreams,
  The noble visionings of high emprise,
The glory of the Grail that brightly gleams
  Across the starry reaches of the skies
And leads us upward from the crumbling clod
Into communion, Lord, with Thee and God.

              —EDGAR DANIEL KRAMER

SONG OF THANKSGIVING

For days gold-bright
That make earth's heart
Beat quick and warm,
For stars of night,
And love that harbors
Me from harm—
I give Thee thanks.

For answered prayers
That stay the soul
And lift and bless,
For grace that bears
With me in hours
Of thanklessness—
I give Thee thanks.

191

O Calvary!—
I never think
Of that red Hill
Or Christ upon the tree,
But that I breathe:
"Love triumphs still!"—
And give Thee thanks.

—JOHN RICHARD MORELAND

A THANKSGIVING TO GOD FOR HIS HOUSE

Lord, Thou hast given me a cell
    Wherein to dwell,
A little house whose humble roof
    Is weatherproof.

. . . .

Low is my porch, as is my fate,
    Both void of state;
And yet the threshold of my door
    Is worn by th' poor
Who thither come and freely get
    Good words or meat.

. . . .

'Tis Thou that crown'st my glittering hearth
    With guiltless mirth.

. . . .

All these, and better Thou dost send
    Me, to this end,
That I should render, for my part,
    A thankful heart.

—ROBERT HERRICK

A PRAYER

Give me work to do;
Give me health;
Give me joy in simple things.
Give me an eye for beauty,
A tongue for truth,
A heart that loves,
A mind that reasons,
A sympathy that understands;
Give me neither malice nor envy,
But a true kindness
And a noble common sense.
At the close of each day
Give me a book,
And a friend with whom
I can be silent.

—Author Unknown

FOR BEAUTY, WE THANK THEE

For all life's beauties, and their beauteous growth;
For nature's laws and Thy rich providence;
For all Thy perfect processes of life;
For the minute perfection of Thy work,
Seen and unseen, in each remotest part;
For faith, and works, and gentle charity;
For all that makes for quiet in the world;
For all that lifts man from his common rut;
For all that knits the silken bond of peace;
For all that lifts the fringes of the night,
And lights the darkened corners of the earth;
For every broken gate and sundered bar;
For every wide-flung window of the soul;

193

For that Thou bearest all that Thou hast made;
We thank Thee, Lord!

—JOHN OXENHAM

WE THANK THEE

For all Thy ministries—
For morning mist, and gently falling dew;
For summer rains, for winter ice and snow;
For whispering wind and purifying storm;
For the reft clouds that show the tender blue;
For the forked flash and long tumultuous roll;
For mighty rains that wash the dim earth clean;
For the sweet promise of the sevenfold bow;
For the soft sunshine, and the still calm night;
For dimpled laughter of soft summer seas;
For latticed splendor of the sea-borne moon;
For gleaming sands, and granite-frontled cliffs;
For flying spume, and waves that whip the skies;
For rushing gale, and for the great glad calm;
For Might so mighty, and for Love so true,
With equal mind
We thank Thee, Lord!

—JOHN OXENHAM

Christmas

From IN MEMORIAM

The time draws near the birth of Christ:
　　The moon is hid; the night is still;
　　The Christmas bells from hill to hill
Answer each other in the mist.

Four voices of four hamlets round,
　　From far and near, on mead and moor,
　　Swell out and fail, as if a door
Were shut between me and the sound:

Each voice four changes on the wind,
　　That now dilate, and now decrease,
　　Peace and goodwill, goodwill and peace,
Peace and goodwill, to all mankind.
　　　　　　　　　　—ALFRED TENNYSON

PERPETUAL CHRISTMAS

The bells their Christmas message send o'er earth,
The message of our blessed Savior's birth.
For one fair day all thoughts of war are drowned
As songs of peace throughout the world resound.

Ah, that throughout the year those bells might ring
In every realm of human trafficking!
That every day in every heart might be
One thought: Good will to all—and charity!
　　　　　　　　　　—ARTHUR GORDON FIELD

195

From CHRISTMAS BELLS

I heard the bells on Christmas Day
Their old, familiar carols play,
    And wild and sweet
    The word repeat
Of peace on earth, good-will to men!

And thought how, as the day had come,
The belfries of all Christendom
    Had rolled along
    The unbroken song
Of peace on earth, good-will to men!

Till, ringing, singing on its way,
The world revolved from night to day,
    A voice, a chime,
    A chant sublime
Of peace on earth, good-will to men!

. . . .

Then pealed the bells more loud and deep:
"God is not dead; nor doth he sleep!
    The Wrong shall fail,
    The Right prevail,
With peace on earth, good-will to men!"
      —HENRY WADSWORTH LONGFELLOW

ALCHEMY

The whole, wide world, turned selfless for a day,
Lays down its gifts beneath the Christmas fir,
And, strangely, touched by memory of a star,
Each gift is gold and frankincense and myrrh.
      —ADELAIDE LOVE

NO SWEETER THING

Life holds no sweeter thing than this—to teach
A little child the tale most loved on earth
And watch the wonder deepen in his eyes
The while you tell him of the Christ Child's birth;

The while you tell of shepherds and a song,
Of gentle, drowsy beasts and fragrant hay
On which that starlit night in Bethlehem
God's tiny Son and his young mother lay.

Life holds no sweeter thing than this—to tell
A little child, while Christmas candles glow,
The story of a Babe whose humble birth
Became the loveliest of truths we know.
—ADELAIDE LOVE

THREE WISE KINGS

To Bethlehem town in the long ago
Three Kings of the East came riding;
Over the plains where the hot sands glow,
And over the mountains deep in snow,
Seeking the King in the manger low—
Three Kings of the East ariding.

To the inn they came, to the common room,
And they bowed them low before Him;
And spices and gold and rare perfume
They piled at His feet in the gathering gloom,
But the Christ-child's eyes lit up the room,
As He smiled at the gray heads o'er Him.

197

Then into the night to their lands afar,
The bells on their camels ringing,
They took their way where the wide plains are;
But gone from the sky was the Christmas star,
And strangely gone were the fears that mar,
While peace in their hearts was singing.

And ever as dawns the Christmas day,
The worn old world goes faring,
Seeking the place where the young Child lay,
Where the Kings of the East bowed low to pray,
And peace was born to abide alway,
In hearts that were long despairing.

—WILLIAM E. BROOKS

From BETHLEHEM-TOWN

Unto a Child in Bethlehem-town
The wise men came and brought the crown;
And while the infant smiling slept,
Upon their knees they fell and wept;
But, with her babe upon her knee,
Naught recked that Mother of the tree,
That should uplift on Calvary
What burthen saveth all and me.

Again I walk in Bethlehem-town,
And think on Him that wears the crown.
I may not kiss His feet again,
Nor worship Him as did I then;
My King hath died upon the tree,
And hath outpoured on Calvary
What blood redeemeth you and me!

—EUGENE FIELD

198

A CHRISTMAS PRAYER

We open here our treasures and our gifts;
And some of it is gold,
And some is frankincense,
And some is myrrh;
For some has come from plenty,
Some from joy,
And some from deepest sorrow of the soul.
But Thou, O God, dost know the gift is love,
Our pledge of peace, our promise of good will.
Accept the gift and all the life we bring.

—HERBERT H. HINES

A CHRISTMAS CAROL

"What means this glory round our feet,"
    The Magi mused, "more bright than morn?"
And voices chanted clear and sweet,
    "Today the Prince of Peace is born!"

"What means that star," the Shepherds said,
    "That brightens through the rocky glen?"
And angels, answering overhead,
    Sang, "Peace on earth, good-will to men!"

'Tis eighteen hundred years and more
    Since those sweet oracles were dumb;
We wait for Him, like them of yore;
    Alas, He seems so slow to come!

But it was said, in words of gold
    No time or sorrow e'er shall dim,
That little children might be bold
    In perfect trust to come to Him.

199

All round about our feet shall shine
  A light like that the wise men saw,
If we our loving wills incline
  To that sweet Life which is the Law.

So shall we learn to understand
  The simple faith of shepherds then,
And, clasping kindly hand in hand,
  Sing, "Peace on earth, good-will to men!"

And they who do their souls no wrong,
  But keep at eve the faith of morn,
Shall daily hear the angel-song,
  "Today the Prince of Peace is born!"

—JAMES RUSSELL LOWELL

NOR HOUSE NOR HEART

Room for all else but love,
In houses and in hearts at Bethlehem.
Does he despair of change,
Who comes to us today as once to them,
But finds us occupied
And unaware and ready to condemn?

Which one shall dare to fling,
Uncalculatingly, his portal wide;
To thrust the trivial out
And bid the late Guest take his ease inside?
Except the Lord Christ come,
Nor house nor heart shall know the Christmastide!

—ELINOR LENNEN

200

IT WAS NOT STRANGE

He came to be The Light,
And so it was not strange
A blazing star should pencil out his path
As Heaven unfurled its glory
On the night!

Wise kings came from afar!
Could aught more fitting be
Than kneeling sovereigns to greet
The King of Kings—sweet Baby
Of their star?

With staffs, and sandal-shod,
The shepherds came to search;
Such gentle men—it was not strange that they
Should find in Bethlehem
The Lamb of God!

—ESTHER LLOYD HAGG

CHILDLIKE HEART

The Christmas star burns overhead
Above our homes tonight;
Its gleaming, golden rays are shed
From stern, majestic height.

Yet even humble doors may part
To let that clear light in,
For Christ has taught the childlike heart
That God and man are kin.

—ELLEN WESTON CATLIN

201

O YEARS UNBORN

O years unborn, what mystery
  Will you reveal to age and youth
From highest height to deepest sea,
  From fettered doubt or wingèd truth?

What songs of steel whose lyric note
  Will make new music for our ears;
What flame from lightning's yellow throat
  To bind us to the alien spheres?

What towering temples built of stone
  Will rise like Babel from the sod
That men by flesh and blood alone
  May climb the heights and walk with God?

But years unborn, not yours to bring
  By fire or sword or stratagem
The gift to make the angels sing . . .
  The star that led to Bethlehem!

        —JOHN RICHARD MORELAND

PILGRIMAGE

Discord and darkness—but the Song and the Star
  Can change our night as it was changed for them
When simple folk and wise men from afar
  Came with their eager need to Bethlehem.

The angels sang to such a world as this;
  In threatening night, the Star shone from above.
A pity if, perplexed in heart, we miss
  The music and the radiance—and the Love!

        —ELINOR LENNEN

202

SONG OF THE WISE MEN

Do you not see the Christmas star,
  The star that walks on high?
Or is the firmament, for you,
  But dark and empty sky?

Do you not hear the angels sing,
  In lucent glory shod?
Who loves a lie can hear them not,
  Nor see the Word of God.

How can the rapture that we know
  Your sluggard hearts enthrall,
Who mark but fodder in the crib,
  But oxen in the stall?

All through the midnight watch the star
  Still paces out the sky.
Do you not see the Christmas star
  That we are guided by?
                    —EDITH LOVEJOY PIERCE

From SAINT PAUL

Lo as some venturer, from his stars receiving
  Promise and presage of sublime emprise,
Wears evermore the seal of his believing
  Deep in the dark of solitary eyes,

. . . .

So even I, and with a pang more thrilling,
  So even I, and with a hope more sweet,
Yearn for the sign, O Christ, of thy fulfilling,
  Faint for the flaming of thine advent feet.
                    —F. W. H. MYERS

A CHRISTMAS PRAYER

"The star stood over where the young child was—"
Only a star was high enough to mark
Thy cradle, O Thou Holy One of earth!
Was bright enough to point men through the dark
Since that glad night of old that saw Thy birth!

For stars belong to the unbounded skies;
Stars are not found beneath the roofs of creed,
Nor reached by straining spires of steel and stone:
Alike they shine to serve a whole world's need,
That none dare cry, "The stars are mine alone!"

O Star beyond all stars, the darkness still
Is slow to comprehend! O Light of men,
The glare of earth has kept us blind so long!
Forgive us as we lift our eyes again,
And make us brave to live the angels' song!
—MOLLY ANDERSON HALEY

NOEL! NOEL!

Oh Christmas, that your Gift of Gifts might be
Amongst us yet! as once in Galilee—
Telling of lilies, and of birds overhead—
Of little children and our daily bread—
To us, His humble fisher-folk! make plain
The shining wonder of Himself again,
That we may touch the seamless garment's rim
And be made whole, through the dear grace of Him!
Across the centuries that seem so far—
How close the Christ Child comes! how near the Star!
—LAURA SIMMONS

204

STAR OF THE EAST

Star of the East, that long ago
  Brought wise men on their way
Where, angels singing to and fro,
  The Child of Bethlehem lay—
Above that Syrian hill afar
Thou shinest out tonight, O Star!

Star of the East, the night were drear
  But for the tender grace
That with thy glory comes to cheer
  Earth's loneliest, darkest place;
For by that charity we see
Where there is hope for all and me.

Star of the East! show us the way
  In wisdom undefiled
To seek that manger out and lay
  Our gifts before the child—
To bring our hearts and offer them
Unto our King in Bethlehem!

—EUGENE FIELD

DAY DAWN OF THE HEART

'Tis not enough that Christ was born
  Beneath the star that shone,
And earth was set that holy morn
  Within a golden zone.
He must be born within the heart
  Before he finds a throne,
And brings the day of love and good,
The reign of Christlike brotherhood.

—AUTHOR UNKNOWN

THE FORGOTTEN STAR

Above a world entrapped by fear
   There shone a silver Star.
The doubters saw it not, nor cared;
   The men of faith, from far,
Knew that the Lord of Love looked down,
And followed it through field and town.

Through desert lands they found their way,
   Past mountains, bleak and wild;
They came to humble Bethlehem
   And found a little Child.
Their hearts rejoiced—their feet had trod
Through desert wastes to learn of God.

Our hearts are broken by the years,
   But still there shines the Star
Above a little manger home.
   O that we might, from far,
Retrace our steps from fear and night
To faith and hope, and Bethlehem's light!

       —Thomas Curtis Clark

"AND LO, THE STAR!"

"And lo, the Star," the changeless, the abiding.
   Across the desert strange new paths are laid,
And men who trusted earth-lights for their guiding
   Stand shuddering at the thing their hands have made.
Is this to be the end of all their dreaming,
   This strewing earth with cities of the dead?
O wise men, wise men, see the Christ Star gleaming
   And follow it to Bethlehem's manger bed!

"And lo, the Star!" Shall desert fears dismay you
Who chart your course beneath its certain light?
Shall pride of race or tongue or creed delay you
When all are equal in the Father's sight?
As long ago they journeyed to adore Him,
The while on stable straw the starlight shone,
O wise men, wise men, lay your hearts before Him
This Holy Night and make His rule your own.
—MOLLY ANDERSON HALEY

IT ISN'T FAR TO BETHLEHEM

Two thousand years are far enough!
Who finds the road to yesterday?
Who bridges gulfs that have no edge—
The past is stars and stars away.

As far away, as far away
As stars are from the light we see,
So far away is Bethlehem
From ticking clocks and you and me.

But on the roads that death ruts deep,
In every cursed and smitten land,
At Christmas Eve or any hour
The beggared ones may find his hand.

For Christ has walked the second mile
Across the years from Bethlehem;
And God's incarnate love still keeps,
In Christ, its comradeship with men.
—ARTHUR R. MACDOUGALL, JR.

207

"HE IS OUR PEACE"

"He is our Peace"—low in a manger lying,
  "He is our Peace," the Day-Spring from on high,
He whom the angel hosts are glorifying
  Draws to himself the far-off and the nigh.
Come, swift as shepherds, to the white light streaming
  From Bethlehem's star to Bethlehem's humble stall;
As wise men, come, let us have done with dreaming,
  There is no Name save his to bind us all.

"He is our Peace"—the Son of God revealing
  The Father's love for all the sons of men:
To broken homes and hearts he comes with healing,
  This Holy Night the Christ Child comes again!
"He is our Peace"—let us have done with stressing
  Our little schemes to shape that world to be,
Scorning all plans that dare not ask his blessing,
  Owning no rule save his can set men free!

—MOLLY ANDERSON HALEY

FROM BETHLEHEM BLOWN

Great is the tumult of men's anger grown,
  Of hate exalted and of love defiled;
But hark, on gentle airs from Bethlehem blown,
  Rise clear the tender accents of a Child!

A little Child—and yet the voice of dread
  Is stilled, greed shamed as wrath and envy are:
Hate's sword is sheathed; the tyrant bows his head,
  As sudden on earth's darkness streams a star!

—MARY SINTON LEITCH

WE HAVE SEEN HIS STAR IN THE EAST

"We have seen His star in the East,"
  In the East where it first stood still,
We have heard the song of the angel throng,
  "And on earth peace, good will!"
But the little lights confuse,
  The nearer sounds obsess,
And our hearts withhold from the Lord of Love
  The lives he would use and bless.

"We have seen His star in the East,"
  His shining dream of the good,
When men shall claim in the Father's name
  Their right to brotherhood.
O little lights, grow dim,
  O nearer sounds, be still,
While our hearts remember Bethlehem,
  And a cross on a far green hill!
        —MOLLY ANDERSON HALEY

EARTH LISTENS

At last our dull Earth listens:
  Peace! Good will!
The Star of Bethlehem glistens
  Nearer, nearer still.

Holy luster christens
  War-torn heath and hill.
At last, at last Earth listens:
  Peace! Good will!
        —KATHARINE LEE BATES

From CHRISTMAS ANTIPHONES

Thou whose birth on earth
Angels sang to men
While thy stars made mirth,
Saviour, at Thy birth
This day born again:

As this night was bright
With thy cradle ray,
Very light of light,
Turn the wild world's night
To thy perfect day.
—ALGERNON C. SWINBURNE

AT CHRISTMASTIDE

How far they throw their cheer, their gracious glow,
The Christmases that happened long ago!
Over what silences they have their way
When hearts come to their own, today!
Each to its secret hoard of gold and myrrh—
Treasured, how long!—from out the years that were:
Old songs, old laughter; still their echoes ring,
Flooding the empty hours with welcoming!
Dear handclasps, swift and warm with ministries—
What matters space, or time, to such as these?
The precious past that none beside can know—
Calling us back, and will not let us go!

O friend, be comforted that memory brings
The gift of changeless, sure and hallowed things!
Closer today they press on every side
Always and always ours, at Christmastide.
—LAURA SIMMONS

COME, HOLY BABE!

Did Bethlehem's stable loathe
Its drab, dull stone?
And did the oxen sense their common lot?
The hay its coarse inadequacy?
The earth-pressed floor, unworthiness?

My heart is shabby, too: ·
Come, Manger Light!
Make my dull spirit glow
This Silent Night!

—MARY DICKERSON BANCHAM

CHRISTMAS PRAYER

Let Christmas not become a thing
Merely of merchants' trafficking,
Of tinsel, bell and holly wreath
And surface pleasure, but beneath
The childish glamor let us find
Nourishment for soul and mind.
Let us follow kinder ways
Through our teeming human maze
And help the age of peace to come
From a Dreamer's martyrdom.

—MADELINE MORSE

ETERNAL CHRISTMAS

In the pure soul, although it sing or pray,
The Christ is born anew from day to day;
The life that knoweth Him shall abide apart
And keep eternal Christmas in the heart.

—ELIZABETH STUART PHELPS

211

From A CHRISTMAS HYMN

It is the calm and solemn night!
A thousand bells ring out and throw
Their joyous peal abroad, and smite
The darkness, charmed and holy now!
The night that erst no name had worn,
To it a happy name is given;
For in that stable lay new-born,
The peaceful Prince of Earth and Heaven,
In the solemn midnight
Centuries ago.
—ALFRED DOMETT

CHRISTMAS EVE

Pine-crowned hills against the sky,
Kneeling low to pray;
Friendly, lamp-lit villages
Along the snowbound way;
Myriads of silver stars
Gleaming softly bright. . . .
Little King of Bethlehem,
I see Thy star tonight!

Fragrant wreaths and candle-glow
In a city street,
Songs of Christmas carolers
High and clear and sweet—
Echoes of the angel host,
With wings of shining white. . . .
Little King of Israel,
I hear Thy song tonight!

212

Words of ancient prophecy
Are mine to take or leave:
Visions of a golden age
This happy Christmas Eve.
Peace on earth, good will to men—
Oh, dim and holy light! . . .
Little King of all the world,
I share Thy dream tonight!

—CATHERINE PARMENTER

THROUGH THE AGES

Peace on the earth,
Joyfully sang the angels long ago;
They could not know
That when two thousand years had rolled their way
The golden age of peace would still delay.

Peace on the earth?
Ah, no—not yet:
The nations of the world are sore beset
With fears and dark unrest; we do not see
Signs of the dawn, the peace that was to be.

Good will to men.
And yet it comes—that day expected long
When earth at length shall hear the Bethlehem song;
When sounds of war in every land shall cease
And men shall own as Lord the Prince of Peace.

O blessèd time!
And so the angel hymns still sweetly chime,
And still on hearts boastful of many locks
The Christ-child knocks.

—MARGARET HOPE

213

CHRISTMAS AMNESTY
Liberty to the captives (Isa. 61:1)

To break bolt and bar,
To open the door,
Requires no more
Than the light of a Star.

For shame, who are we
Its message to mock—
To shutter the lock
From the Christmas key?

—EDITH LOVEJOY PIERCE

NOEL

How blessèd were Judean hills
    Whose lonely rock-strewn height
Reflected glory from the skies
    Upon that holy night!

How blessèd were the shepherds
    Who heard the angels sing!
How blessèd was the manger
    Which held the promised King!

How blessèd were the Magi and
    The star that guided them!
And blessèd are all hearts today
    Which turn toward Bethlehem.

—GAIL BROOK BURKET

214

THE LORD OF THE WORLD

Come sail with me o'er the golden sea
To the land where the rainbow ends,
Where the rainbow ends,
And the great earth bends
To the weight of the starry sky,
Where the tempests die with a last fierce cry,
And never a wind is wild.
There's a Mother mild, with a little Child
Like a star set on her knee;
When bow you down, give him the crown—
'Tis the Lord of the World you see.
—G. A. STUDDERT-KENNEDY

DECEMBER 26

Chants, incense, and the glory pass and die:
  The festive lights diminish; solemn prayer
Gives way to ribald song and pageantry,
  And market cries again confuse the square.

And he whose spirit held us for one day,
  Seeing love consumed again by doubt and fear,
Sorrowing, returns the long and thorny way
  Until we make him welcome through the year.
—GEORGE EDWARD HOFFMAN

Indexes

Index of Authors

222

Index of Titles

228

233

234

Index of First Lines

Father, I will not ask for wealth or fame, 20
Flowers for you, O Glory's son, war's prey! 106
For all life's beauties, and their beauteous growth, 193
For all the wonders of this wondrous world, 185
For all Thy ministries, 194
For days gold-bright, 191
For glowing autumn's brimming yield, 188
For I dipped into the future, far as human eye could see, 172.
For others she may not be fair, 83
From Bethlehem to Calvary the Savior's journey lay, 44
Full many are the centuries since the days, 60

Give me work to do, 193
Give thanks, O heart, for the high souls, 151
God of our lives, O hear our prayer, 21
God of the seasons, hear my parting prayer, 13
God thought to give the sweetest thing, 80
Golgotha's journey is an ancient way, 47
Good Friday in my heart! Fear and affright! 46
Great is the tumult of men's anger grown, 208

Hail, guest! We ask not what thou art, 132
Hats off! 115
Haughty they said he was, at first, severe, 37
"Have ye founded your thrones and altars, then," 140
He came not as the princes born to rule, 27
He came to be The Light, 201
He came to my desk with a quivering lip, 15
He gave his life upon the cross, 47
"He is our Peace"—low in a manger lying, 208
He who plants a tree, 76
Heap high the board with plenteous cheer and gather to the feast, 185
Hear me, my warriors; my heart is sick and sad, 154
Her hands have much, 86
Here in this simple house his presence clings, 25

242